Economical Growth

Chris Pham

DEDICATION

To mom, dad and sister.

CONTENTS

SHOUT OUTS

Family first. Mom and dad, who are my inspirations. You two are a vision of everything I hope to one day become. My sister, Paulina, is always there with kindness and giving.

I'd also like to thank my editors and contributors. Edan Rubin, Amanda Arthur and Ailbhe Rees are each rock stars who went out of their way to develop the concepts within this book. Dan Ahmadi and Nima Haghighi worked diligently as trusted partners to stand everything up in operation.

I am also very grateful to my managers and mentors, people who have opened doors for me and challenged me to become better. Ian Black, Simon Parmett and Carl Tsukahara in particular.

I have to mention The Phamily of ISRs, ADRs and SDRs. I couldn't have done any of this without you. The 6am Skype chats, the late nights practicing pitches, the bad idea Napa wine buses, the hire 2x in 2 month goals, the tears of relief/joy/disbelief, the about-to-crush-this-meeting looks and the delirious Christmas Eve laughs we share mean everything to me. Our success follows naturally in the wake of your indomitable spirit.

Most notably, Kim Dill, Stephanie Leetham, Brigid Fox, Steven Broudy, Matt Duffy and Seth Olsen…thanks for always bringing the fire.

Lastly, a huge shout out to you, the reader. Kick ass and take names, my friend.

INTRODUCTION

You've cracked open (or more likely, tapped open) this book because you need growth.

Whether you're a CEO, Head of Sales, VP of Marketing, Sales Development Leader or Investor, you're looking at the highly competitive enterprise B2B market and want to determine your company's fate.

And beyond simple growth, you want to create **economical** growth - a solid foundation to a sound company. In the frothy markets of Silicon Valley, where user count or a few downloads will earn multi-million dollar valuations, growth for growth's sake is often viewed as gold. But losing money to make money is not a real long-term strategy.

Economical growth delivers predictable revenue linearly **and** at a profit.

Professional Sales Development will not only deliver economical growth, but will do so at scale. It can be as ambitious as your billion-dollar dreams; millions are the aspirations of the uninspired.

> "I want to build a brick house."
> - Doug Leone
> Managing Partner, Sequoia Capital

Professionally executed Sales Development offers a path to building billion-dollar value, brick by brick. With it, you can construct a quality company that is healthy from the inside out.

First, I want to acknowledge the great work and core foundation laid by Aaron Ross and Mary Lou Tyler in *Predictable Revenue*. Without them, Sales Development would not exist today.

Predictable Revenue theorizes correctly that dividing the labor of sales into multiple parts (namely prospecting and closing) achieves optimal efficiency for the sales organization. *Economical Growth* seeks to professionalize the prospecting function in the age of the Millennial, to deliver 10x returns.

Furthermore, where *Predictable Revenue* takes place in early 2000s, this book will put you in 2016, in a time when the buyer has been empowered more than ever and a new generation of knowledge worker has fundamentally changed the expectations inside the workplace.

With this book you can plan, manage and execute a modern, enterprise Sales Development vision at Unicorn scale.

ECONOMICAL GROWTH

CHAPTER 1
BE THE LIGHT

In this chapter we explore my personal experience as it relates to Sales Development.

Part 1: Finding Sales Development
Part 2: Of Mules and Unicorns

Part 1: Finding Sales Development

I found Sales Development by accident. Really, Sales Development found me.

As a fresh Wharton graduate in 2010, I moved to Silicon Valley with little more than an old TV, my parent's couch and the hope to join an industry that was going to make a positive difference in the world. We were still in the aftermath of the 2008 financial meltdown, and I headed West to avoid the "great vampire squid wrapped around the face of humanity", as *Rolling Stone* described the banking industry.

Ever since I was a kid, I have been interested in technology. Whether it was building computers or playing DOOM, there was an air of constant innovation, excitement, learning and most of all…fun that surrounded technology. And there is nowhere in the world more at the center of that world than San Francisco.

Shortly after arriving in SF, Autonomy (later acquired by HP) hired me to run their North American inside sales and sales development team. I'll never forget the spot-offer from then-CMO Nicole Eagan; she offered me a position managing a dozen salespeople when I was only a year out of university! Quite a break for a 22 year-old kid. Soon, I was managing 30 sales reps in 3 cities, and I earned my stripes quickly (if not dearly).

During those years, when faced with a difficult challenge, I would turn to my father for advice (and still do). One of the boat people from the Vietnam War, he had clawed his way up to leading 300 engineers as VP of Engineering at Motorola, only later to trade in those 15 years in the corporate world to become a dentist (to more directly help people, he says).

His guidance is powerful - if brief:

"Be the light."

So that's what I tried to do for those at Autonomy, help my people get the most out of themselves. And it worked.

In the first year, our team cracked $40M of sourced business. The next year, we did $80M. The power of a highly functional sales development framework was on full display.

The combination of developing talent, and the dramatic influence that could make had a profound effect on me. To grow young professionals - to be the light - <u>and</u> to be able to make a huge, quantifiable difference to the company had me hooked.

Part 2: Of Mules and Unicorns

By early 2013 the flood of venture capital that had receded with the Great Recession had come roaring back into Silicon Valley and - more specifically - San Francisco itself. One of the companies that benefited from the timing was MuleSoft – valued at $400M at the time I joined in January 2013. MuleSoft faced a familiar problem – they had a solid product and were looking to disrupt legacy vendors by moving up-market. In this case, they had the advantage of being cloud-based while the old guns were all on premise.

We've seen this movie before, most notably Salesforce's domination of Siebel and Workday's aggressive push against PeopleSoft. Regardless of the exact circumstance, when you need to unseat a competitor you need to provide your salespeople with a foothold strong enough to displace old relationships, long lunches and entrenched interests.

To create these opportunities, I developed a scalable Account-Based Sales Development (ABSD) model.

I was hired to build the Sales Development organization when MuleSoft barely had 100 employees. In the beginning, we had 5 SDRs based in London and San Francisco.

In the next three years SDRs would expand to Atlanta, Singapore, Sydney and Buenos Aires -- totaling to over 60 individual contributors and 8 managers covering 11 languages in 6 cities.

But more than the growth, SDRs at MuleSoft produced results. Sales Development was the only source of business that the company could consistently count on. Our group sourced the vast majority of the company's new and add-on revenue, while **doubling** that base each year **for three consecutive years.**

Additionally, we promoted 20 SDRs into positions in management, marketing, customer success, operations and field sales. The SDRs were a consistent pipeline of talent for the company to draw upon.

In that short span, the pipeline increased 10x and predictably turned into revenue.

By 2016, MuleSoft made the jump. During the fiscal year of 2015, MuleSoft booked over $100M of revenue[1]. We were on Fortune's Unicorn List – valued at over $1.5Bn – and swollen to over 900 customers including global brands AT&T, Unilever, Siemens, Verizon and Mastercard. The fuel for the growth behind that customer base and valuation, the foundation and core, was Sales Development.

Greg Schott, MuleSoft's CEO, stands behind Sales Development as the cornerstone to his billion-dollar business, "[SDRs] have been the engine room for the company…we would not be where we are today without the team."

---

[1] http://www.zdnet.com/article/mulesoft-crosses-100-million-revenue-mark/

CHAPTER 2
THE RISE OF SALES DEVELOPMENT

Sales Development has become a critical function for growth companies to get right. In this chapter we explore why and the state of the industry today.

Part 1: The Growing Chasm
Part 2: A Declaration of Independence
Part 3: Sales Development Leadership, the Profession
Part 4: The Case for Enterprise Tech Sales
Part 5: ABSD and The Death of Inbound/Outbound

Part 1: The Growing Chasm

Geoffrey Moore's classic *Crossing the Chasm* details the gap in adoption of cutting-edge products. Published in 2006, the chasm is real and has only grown harder to bridge over time.

The gap has widened as buyer power has increased – as evidenced by the rise of Gartner and Forrester. This has been further exacerbated by the increase in information flooding the consumer market, driving similar expectations into the enterprise.

Think of the last time you went to purchase anything – a quick Google or Amazon search for reviews and pricing is now standard operating procedure. To decide on which burrito to eat in San Francisco, you might consult EaterSF, Yelp, a half-dozen food blogs, your best foodie friend, or ask your co-worker who just came back with a burrito from the truck down the street. And that's just your decision-making process for lunch. Imagine when it's a multi-million dollar purchase and your career on the line.

Our fundamental expectation on the value and information vendors must provide continues to expand. Customers expect detailed product information, comparisons, expert reviews, and a point-of-view on usage. And that's all before they engage with a vendor in purchasing. SiriusDecisions states that prospects complete 67% of their journey digitally[2].

The core of professional Account-Based Sales Development aims to provide enough value to business prospects in order to *earn the right to engage earlier*. And, once engaged, to set-up sales in a winning position for the initial conversation.

Doing so creates deterministic demand within a controllable ideal target profile (ITP), a profile that will act with consistency and convert at scale. ABSD creates demand that will steadily, but surely, bridge Moore's chasm.

---

[2] http://www.ontargetconference.com/wp-content/uploads/2014/03/2_SiriusDecisions_On-Target_2014_Vendemore_event.pdf

Part 2: A Declaration of Independence

Historically, Sales Development has been the redheaded stepchild of the business – in turn it reports into Marketing, Sales or Operations. No one really knows where the function fits in. In reality, Sales Development is its own discipline – that is why it doesn't fit in anywhere.

Sales Development requires skills that the other organizations do not possess, namely the ability to create and qualify demand, and to develop and recruit young professionals.

Yet Sales Development suffers middle-child syndrome not from a lack of importance – as we've seen at MuleSoft, the department can be critical to the success of successful companies – but a lack of leadership and maturity from within the Sales Development industry itself.

World-class pipeline generation at scale necessitates strong leadership from an independent Sales Development function. At MuleSoft, Sales Development reported into the SVP of Field Operations - just like Sales, Customer Success, Partners, and Services. As business recognize the importance of Sales Development, reporting directly to a C-level will become the industry standard. And as the industry matures and professionalizes, reporting directly to the CEO will become more and more common.

We should and do declare Independence for the profession of Sales Development.

Side Note: Revolution! Inside Sales v. Sales Development

Inside Sales has traditionally encapsulated both Sales Development and Inside Sales, but this banner is misleading and detrimental.

Sales Development is an entirely different animal, one which focuses on prospecting at scale, qualifying and creating engagement.

Closing business is entirely different than creating business, so we should leave the moniker of Inside Sales to those who close business without leaving the confines of their offices.

Part 3: Sales Development Leadership, the Profession

There's a direct analogy between college football (the American type) and sales development. There was a time not too long ago where college football coaches were seen as coaches-in-training for the NFL. College football was a breeding ground, a time for coaches to prove they could produce - that they could run a team.

But as college football matured, it became its own industry with its own unique challenges. Coaches in the NFL didn't have to deal with boosters, parents, local high schools and young professionals early in their development. There was value in the Nick Saban's of the world, who could identify, recruit, coach and grow high-school talent into NFL-ready players.

Today, Coach Saban is paid more than most NFL coaches ($7 million a year). College Coaches are choosing to stay in their profession for the duration of their careers, regularly turning down coaching vacancies in the NFL. We are entering a similar transition in Sales Development.

Personally, what drives me is recruiting, teaching, challenging and witnessing the growth of young professionals. Raw talent, with that internal fire - that chip on their shoulder - is the clay with which Sales Development leaders work. Sales Development leaders bring this talent to the highly lucrative – but under-marketed – profession of enterprise technology sales.

In order to predictably create demand and scale companies, Sales Development needs professional management and it should become a profession in and of itself. Traditionally viewed as a temporary position (or passed between functions), there is a dearth of talent in Sales Development leadership because of its supposed transient nature.

"Don't waste your skills in Sales Development."

That mentality is so wrong because it fundamentally underestimates the impact of the function. The skills needed to be great at Sales

Development management are related to, but very different from, those needed in Sales, Marketing or Operations. And to develop those skills requires an understanding and acceptance that Sales Development leadership is a **career** – a calling to develop All-Star caliber talent and to build the growth engine in enterprise technology companies.

Sales Development managers have the opportunity to impact the growth of the next generation of industry leaders – at a time in their lives when they are most open to learning. Having that impact on their trajectory should drive Sales Development coaches every day.

Side Note: The Story of Brigid
One outstanding example of the power of Sales Development to shape the leaders of tomorrow is the story of a hard-headed but highly motivated SDR out of London, Brigid.

She would always crush her quota and lead the pack - but sometimes to the detriment of bruising others. Together, we worked hard to identify and work on the skills she needed to deliver with excellence while still positively impacting those around her. We spoke about communication styles, emotional intelligence and active listening.

In the succeeding years, Brigid went on to manage a SDR team and then to an enterprise closing role where she continued to kill her quota using the same skills she learned and worked on as an SDR.

A typical Sales coach wouldn't have the infrastructure or process necessary to bring out the best of someone with such great, but unrefined potential. Most importantly, field Sales leaders don't have the *time*. Their need to produce revenue today far outweighs the investment necessary to allow someone like Brigid to become an all-star tomorrow. *But Sales Development does have the time.*

Just before winning the 2016 College Football Playoff National Championship, Nick Saban reflected on his development philosophy,

"We try to get our guys to focus on what do [they] need to do to be a complete player...where can [they] be the best player three years from now."[3]

Coach Saban has the time to develop his players into the champions of today and the professionals of tomorrow. So does Sales Development.

And just like college football coaches, Sales Development leaders are more than the plays and tactics on the field. They are more than the X's and O's, the calls and emails.

SDR leaders are educators, facilitators, mentors, coaches, team-builders and career launchers...they are the ones shaping the next generation of tech talent and fueling some of the largest companies in the world.

They should be proud to do so.

Sales Development leadership has become so specialized that it should become a profession in it's own right. The power of Sales Development has been a competitive advantage for SaaS companies for the past decade, but it has now become a necessity as the broader market has adopted the business model. Simply having a Sales Development team is now table stakes.

To continue to drive a competitive advantage, Sales Development needs mature and professional leadership.

---

[3] http://www.cw.ua.edu/article/2016/01/coaches-focus-on-developing-players-for-life

Part 4: The Case for Enterprise Tech Sales

What other entry-level job can lead directly to a career where you can earn $1,000,000 every year?

Historically, "de facto" lucrative professions – like banking, accounting, law and private equity – attract our nation's finest. The have legions of recruiters and a talent pipeline direct from universities that allows them to take advantage of talented, young labor. They've enabled themselves to do so by developing intensive and rigorous training programs - something Sales Development could take a lesson from.

In many ways, the perception of Sales is that of a job of last resort - one which provides little value, limited stability, and conjures thoughts of the used car salesman - and that must change.

In reality, there's a **reason** you can make $1M+ per year in enterprise tech sales; it **demands** you provide value. Tech sales works in a fast-paced, competitive environment where you have to provide value in order to survive. Unlike other industries, it doesn't rely on laws or regulations. Business is earned every day by creating value and innovation above the next vendor, in a hyper-competitive and egalitarian world.

With the rise of new sales methodologies like CEB's *The Challenger Sale*, even the sales cycles (and therefore salespeople) are designed to provide value to customers. Sales is no longer the smile-and-dial jobs of the past. Now, enterprise technology sales involves a deep knowledge of technical components, an understanding of complex business environments and an ability to communicate effectively.

Enterprise tech sales is a new combination of geek, analyst, teacher and consultant. And Sales Development is where you get started.

Sophisticated Buyer

Luxury Travel/Goods
Sales Development

Enterprise Technology
Sales Development

Low Skill

High Skill

Consumer Technology
Sales Development

SMB Technology
Sales Development

Unsophisticated Buyer

Part 5: ABSD and The Death of Inbound/Outbound

Sales Development has traditionally come from a world focused on the process of optimizing a lead. A lead typically means someone who has expressed interest...a contact form on a website, a trial started or an asset downloaded. SDRs follow-up in the least time possible, diagnose the need and close for a meeting. If they're not doing that, then they're cold calling people to drum up demand. In this traditional world, the one we've been living in for decades, there's inbound and outbound.

That is no longer true in today's world. Every enterprise B2B company needs to kill the notion of inbound and outbound.

A B2B company shouldn't care if a prospect came to the SDR or the SDR goes to the prospect - what matters is the methodology and value they engage the prospect with, and how effectively they're setting the stage for the AE.

Instead, enterprise Sales Development should move to Account-Based Sales Development (ABSD). Seeing the world in in/outbound terms frames the world in a salesperson's eyes, with notions like "this lead is coming to me" or "I'm approaching her." This is a self-centered view of the world, which doesn't help in doing the core job: creating demand in the company's ideal target profile.

In order to successfully penetrate the B2B enterprise market, companies have to employ ABSD. ABSD is a tactic specific to B2B enterprise sales because of the complexity of selling to large enterprise accounts and the depth necessary to earn credibility with sophisticated buyers. In high-velocity B2C sales development models, traditional lead processing with a focus on high-volume throughput may be the preferred option. That sales model is not explored in this book.

Instead, let's focus on the enterprise software space. Using the ABSD model, SDRs should treat each lead, wherever it has come from, as an idea. **A lead is a clue** as to which accounts may fall into the ideal target profile and which accounts/contacts are worth their time to further develop. They point to potential transformation or initiatives within an account, guiding SDRs to craft a meaningful and provocative point-of-view (PPOV) which can be used to differentiate from the competition and engage the prospect in meaningful discussion.

The development and penetration of each account lies with providing insightful value by doing research to understand the prospect's environment, business challenges, and providing industry context on how your solution has previously been applied and to what end. This is the PPOV and by consistently delivering it SDRs earn time with prospects.

The Challenger Sale teach, tailor and take control methodology has fundamentally changed prospecting. The old in/outbound paradigm assumes marketing has done most of the lift and simply checks the turkey to see if it's fully cooked, i.e. if a project has been started yet. This will not work when the competition is moving to engage earlier than ever by teaching, tailoring and taking control.

Sales has become more Challenging

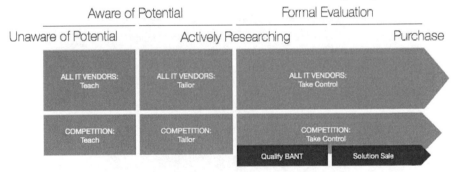

The competition is not only other vendors in your space, but all Enterprise software vendors. They are all executing on Challenger Sale and driving our prospect's business priorities.

Using ABSD, SDRs now have to understand a prospect's business and technology so well as to surprise and delight them with insightful analysis and new ideas **before** they are aware of a problem. SDRs need to teach their prospects how they could potentially improve their business.

Move into the Teacher's Seat

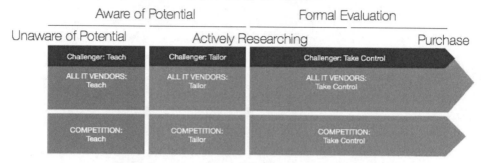

You can win by being in the teacher's seat, by proactively engaging all our prospects with valuable, surprising insights which beat the quality provided all the other vendors, a difficult but necessary task to win.

Furthermore, with the in/outbound paradigm there are only so many prospects who are innovative enough to self-realize their own need; these are Moore's innovators. The problem is that there are not very many of them in the world.

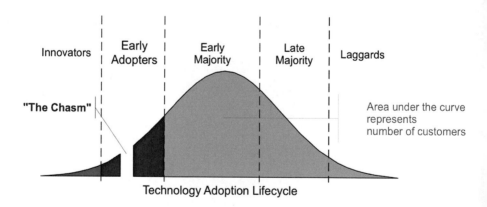

Technology Adoption Lifecycle

With ABSD, using *The Challenger Sale* principles from CEB, SDRs can be the frontline to teach the early adopters and the early majority, a much larger portion of the market. They are laying the first cables to bridge the gap.

Although in/outbound is dead, it is still critical to differentiate two different roles within Sales Development, *though they are no longer inbound and outbound.*

The Account Development and Market Development roles are needed to create a scalable way to manage territories, align with the field and, most of all, to create focus.

Account Development (ADRs) – focus on developing and penetrating roughly 100 accounts at a time.

Market Development (MDRs) – focus on maximizing account penetration within a geographic territory using each lead as an idea.

Both ADRs and MDRs should receive leads *and* go outbound to create demand.

In this way, ABSD is best done in a hybrid model.

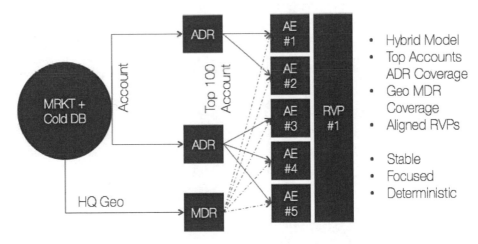

Typically ADRs will receive a minimal amount of leads (many of which they have driven to the website themselves through their outbound work), while MDRs receive the bulk of marketing's efforts. Though hopefully this changes as Marketing teams get better at Account-Based Marketing (ABM).

The hybrid model creates straightforward field and sales development alignment, essential to building the teaming necessary to intelligently penetrate accounts.

It is especially critical for MDRs to reframe this in/outbound discussion. Doing so will fundamentally redefine their role as a hybrid function. This new definition gives MDRs complete territory ownership which empowers them to develop contacts in accounts that would otherwise be left dormant.

In the world defined by in/outbound – MDRs would process leads and the specific contact which comes with it. If a low level contact from Visa came in as a lead, MDRs would follow-up. In the perfect world, he would put 6 or more touches on the lead, and then would quickly move on to the next lead.

With ABSD, MDRs have complete ownership of the geographic market (less accounts owned by ADRs) and are empowered with the autonomy to pursue each lead as they see fit. MDRs are free to engage new accounts and contacts in ways that typical inbound reps would not or could not before. They can now focus on using their leads as clues in order to craft their penetration strategies and attack their accounts holistically.

Now, using the same low level lead from Visa would guide a MDR to craft a PPOV that can be delivered to that specific contact *and* all of the other contacts in the account that could mobilize a project. The MDR has been freed to thoughtfully attack Visa from all available angles.

Side Note: Focus the number of Accounts
An individual ADR should be focused on about 100 accounts per quarter. As we first deployed the ABSD, we knew that the number of accounts an ADR should own needed to be studied. In 2013, a straw poll of Sales Development leaders responded with a range between 10 and 500 accounts -- with no real data to back-up why.

So for one year beginning in 2014, we allowed 7 ADRs to own up to 300 accounts and 7 ADRs to own 120. During this year, the entire team averaged over 100% of quota. We then looked at the data - tens of thousands of touches across thousands of accounts.

The results weren't terribly surprising. The ADRs with 300 accounts watched a slow drip of inbound leads that could get them close to quota, but they never did the work to provide account-based messaging. Left to their own devices, they defaulted to the intellectually lazy tactic of spray and pray. This was not only lazy, but ran against the core principle of providing value to our prospects and it burned a lot of accounts.

What we found was that no ADRs had touched more than 100 accounts with over 5+ touches in any quarter. Once the number of accounts narrowed, so too did the focus on account-based messaging and value.

CHAPTER 3
THE SALES DEVELOPMENT MODEL

As a graduate of Wharton, I can't do anything without a financial model. A model will keep Marketing, Sales Development, Sales and Finance aligned on goals, planning and resourcing. Every year you should build or update your Sales Development model. It is the foundation of your business and justifies spend to the CEO/CFO with a clear cost-benefit.

A robust model consists of 3 parts, all focused on triangulating SDR goals, cost and headcount (HC). However, you will see that creating the model will force the business to confront larger truths about its assumptions. As Sales Development sits at the core of the business' ability to generate revenue, the health of the business will quickly become apparent.

The first and most important part of the model consists of a top-down approach focused on revenue. The second model predicts market demand and the HC necessary to meet it. And the third model places a golden ratio in SDR to AE resourcing.

Part 1: The Top-Down Model
Part 2: The Sales Support Model & Golden Ratio
Part 3: The Lead Capacity Model
Part 4: The SDR Multiple

Part 1: The Top-Down Model

For this approach you will need to have the following information or make educated assumptions on them. The process of coming to agreement with critical stakeholders on core assumptions is valuable in and of itself. There are 7 key assumptions:

1. Company Revenue Targets
2. SDR sourced (%)
3. Average Selling Price (ASP)
4. Average Deal Length
5. Close Rate (from Stage 1)
6. # of Opportunities Sourced per SDR
7. # of SDR Head Count (HC)

The formula to optimize is relatively straightforward.

$$CompanyRevenueTarget * SDRsourced = ASP * CloseRate * OppsPerSDR * SDRHeadCount$$

So let's take a quick shot at this with a hypothetical company - **Unicorn Dash**. Unicorn Dash has 2 SDRs that, on average, produce 30 opportunities each per quarter. They expect the MRKT/SDR team to source 60% of new business. Unicorn Dash is moving up market and just crossed the six-figure deal mark; Average Selling Price (ASP) is $100k. It usually takes us 3 months to close a deal.

7 Key Assumptions	Unicorn Dash
Company Revenue Target	New and Add-On Targets - ($12M)
	Q1 – $2M
	Q2 – $3M
	Q3 – $2M
	Q4 – $5M
SDR Sourced %	60%
Average Selling Price (ASP)	$100,000
Average Deal Length	3 Months (1 Qtr.)
Close Rate	10%
# of Opps per SDR (per Q)	30
AE Quota (per Year)	$1M

The company is building the model in November, looking to their targets for next year.

Example: Unicorn Dash - Q1 SDR HC Needed

Unicorn Dash has a $2M target for Q1, 60% of which needs to be sourced by SDRs, or $1.2M. **Note how Unicorn Dash needs to recognize $2M of revenue in Q1, which means that they need to source that in Q4 of the year prior to account for their 3-month Average Deal Length.**

$$\$1.2M sourced(in Q4) = \$100K ASP * 10PCTCloseRate * 30Opportunities * SDRHeadCount$$

SDR HeadCount (in Q4) = $1.2M/300,000
SDR HeadCount (in Q4) = 4

But wait…Unicorn Dash is already behind! It's November and they have 2 fully ramped SDRs…but they need 4 to hit their Q1 targets!

This is a common problem without a fully realized model. A lack of planning will lead to a lack of resourcing will lead to the company missing its target. You can predictably scale revenue and demand with Sales Development, but you have to be forward looking enough to plan for it.

Without a thorough understanding of the business and the expectations for the next year, you cannot predictably plan for explosive growth. And as the sales cycle increases, so too does the need for predictive planning earlier and earlier.

Using the same math across the year, we can see how the team needs to scale.

Example: Unicorn Dash - Fully Ramped HC Model

Q4: 4 SDRs
Q1: 6 SDRs
Q2: 4 SDRs
Q3: 10 SDRs

Note that because the revenue targets use a step-function growth pattern, the headcount tied to the model may similarly rise and fall. It is not optimal to be reducing headcount only to ramp it back up in the next quarter - hiring, training, morale and team consistency would all suffer. Productive SDRs are the fuel to the engine of growth, think of any extra capacity as goodness.

Secondarily, extra capacity can be a buffer for attrition that will ensure you hit your number. A good sales development organization will naturally have high-attrition, the role is at max a 3 year commitment and the most successful SDRs will move even quicker into new roles. This "Talent Tax" needs to be accounted for in planning head-count and capacity, for which I typically give an extra 20%.

Be aware of the impact of increasing sales cycles. As B2B technology companies begin to cross the chasm, the natural and most economical strategy rests in moving to selling toward the enterprise. This elephant hunting allows companies to gain scale without increasing the cost of sale as dramatically.

However, creating and prosecuting demand in the Enterprise market takes far longer than their more nimble counterparts in the SMB market. Sales cycles in the Enterprise generally average from 6 to 12 months, whereas 3 to 6 months or shorter can be the norm for a high velocity SMB model.

What this means, though, is a fundamental shift in planning – companies looking to break into the Enterprise market must understand their needs and invest earlier than ever before. With ramp time for an SDR averaging 5 months in the industry (we'll discuss how to reduce this later), planning needs to happen a full year ahead of revenue recognition to account for the 6 month sales cycle as well.

This can be difficult, especially when growth companies pivot often. However, the move to the enterprise requires commitment and a steady hand. It's an investment.

Sales Development can be economical in the SMB and Enterprise space – the velocity of the model simply forces the throughput necessary. This, in turn, will drive quota (which will be explored in detail in Part II of the book).

Part 2: The Sales Support Model & Golden Ratio

The AE to SDR relationship is the most important professional relationship for SDRs. Account Executives are the customers, mentors, strategists and partners. Developing long-lasting relationships is critical to a SDRs success. This helps them to understand an AE's qualification criteria, business, method of engagement and strategy. A good working relationship will benefit both parties.

It is impossible for an SDR to invest in four or more AE relationships. They will be spread too thin. Secondarily, it is usually not enough production to fill an AE's pipeline if you split an SDR's production into more than 3-4 parts. The following formula will help you determine the ratio necessary to support the field:

$$AEsperSDR = (ASP * CloseRate * OppsSourcedperSDR) \div (AEQuota * SDRSupportPCT)$$

Example: Unicorn Dash - AE-SDR Ratio

Unicorn Dash has an average AE quota of $1M. Assuming everything else stays constant...

$$AEsperSDR = (100KASP * 10PCTCloseRate * 120OppsperSDR) \div (\$1MQuota * 60PCTSDR)$$

\# of AEs per SDR = $1,200,000 / $600,000
\# of AEs per SDR = 2/1

We see that in order to support the field with our current assumptions we will need a 2:1 ratio.

But remember, Unicorn Dash has 10 AEs – meaning that we'd need 5 SDRs to support street quota at the desired mix. This AE forecast and ratio forms one more data-point to triangulate headcount (but is not the end-all).

In Part 1 the model only dictated 4 SDRs on staff by Q1 – but Unicorn Dash needs 5 SDRs to immediately support the field! This difference is usually indicative of over-hiring AEs, although it can be caused from other factors (like a need to adjust assumptions).

Should Unicorn Dash be unable to resource to the 2:1 ratio, we can either increase SDR productivity (i.e. quota) or choose to support only selected reps who need pipeline.

Generally, the Golden Ratio should **not be any larger than 4:1** as SDRs become combat ineffective with too many customers to serve, strategies to remember and accounts to manage.

Part 3: The Lead Capacity Model

The last model centers on servicing the number of Marketing Qualified Leads (MQLs). Look at your data to understand how many MQLs an average SDR can handle each month. As the definition of MQLs vary company by company, this can be a moving target. Typically, the number of MQLs an SDR can handle rests between 3-400 MQLs per month. Your demand-generation team should produce their own yearly MQL forecast, and it is simple division to find the minimum SDR headcount to service the market.

$$MinMarketResponseHC = TotalMQLspermonth \div 300MQLsperSDRperMonth$$

At Unicorn Dash, we're currently receiving 1800 MQLs per month. Easy math:

Example: Unicorn Dash - Lead Capacity Model

$$MinMarketResponseHC = 1800MQLspermonth \div 300MQLsperSDRperMonth$$

Minimum MR SDR HC = 6 MR SDRs

However, be aware that this only serves the market and does not leave any time for generating deterministic demand.

Part 4: The SDR Multiple

Lastly, building out cost budgeting for the group will help you and other executives understand the anticipated cost of running the SDR business. Typically, the largest cost resides in compensation.

$$ICCompensationCost = HC * AverageOTE * ExpectedQuotaPerformance$$

On average, SDRs will find a way to quota (or close to it) and performance usually varies between 80-120%. The best indicator of future performance is past performance, so take a look at your data to model expected performance for the next year.

In addition to Compensation, take into account other costs like management compensation and operating costs (like tooling, SPIFFs and travel).

$$TotalCost = ICComp + MGMTComp + OperatingCosts$$

Once all of these are tallied, you can find the SDR Multiple, or the ratio between revenue sourced and the cost to develop that revenue.

$$SDRMultiple = RevenueSourced \div TotalCost$$

Let's put it all together now to find the SDR Multiple at Unicorn Dash. Since Unicorn Dash has a 3 month sales cycle, they now need to look into Q1 of the year after next in order to understand how much revenue to source in the upcoming year.

Example: Unicorn Dash - SDR Multiple

Unicorn Dash New and Add-On Targets - ($14M)

~~Q1 – 2M~~
Q2 – 3M
Q3 – 2M
Q4 – 5M
Q1 - 4M
Total = $14M

Our assumption was that SDR's account for 60% of the $14M total, or $8.4M of revenue.

Let's say that the executive team at Unicorn Dash decided to support the financial model in Part 1 and they've smoothed out the headcount so we're not hiring or firing in a reactive manner.

Assuming each SDR costs $100K per year ($25K per quarter):

Smoothed HC and SDR IC Cost Schedule - Unicorn Dash

Q1: 6 SDRs = $150K
Q2: 6 SDRs = $150K
Q3: 10 SDRs = $250K
Q4: 10 SDRs = $250K
Total IC Compensation = $800K

MGMT Compensation = $150K
Operating Budget = $50K
Total Cost = $1M

$$SDRMultiple = \$8.4MRevenueSourced \div \$1MTotalCost$$

$$SDRMultiple = 8.4x$$

Wow! So you can see that at Unicorn Dash, if you invest $1 into the SDR machine, it turns into $8.4 in revenue. And as the organization scales, the multiple should increase.

Teams that are run efficiently can generate higher multiples as they mature; they become more productive and need less management. Additionally, as SDR teams grow they enjoy economies of scale and diminishing cost of pooled resources. Mature teams are also spending less time tweaking the target profile and developing the right process. Rather, they are more focused on scaling execution, which should boost productivity.

A target SDR Multiple of 10x represents the baseline for a lean and well-run SDR organization.

The SDR Multiple states that for every $1 invested in the SDR organization there's a return of $10 of revenue. Not bad!

Let's reiterate the power of this statement, because it is one of the most powerful principles of Sales Development. SDRs are a consistent, predictable method to scale growth linearly, at a 10x rate.

One dollar of SDR spend will result in ten dollars of sourced revenue...and it only gets better over time.

An effective and consistently performing SDR program executing on Account-Based Sales Development gives companies the confidence to continue investing in themselves and a clear path to growth. It safely forms the foundation of a direct-sale business, allowing the organization to explore other revenue channels as well.

Sales Development is a foundational discipline that can and will have a tremendous impact on every enterprise software organization.

Now that the potential value of ABSD is clear, we will move on to learn how to execute ABSD to drive economical growth. The devil, after all, is in the details.

CHAPTER 4
BUILDING AN ALL-STAR TEAM

The long-term success of your Sales Development team depends on the ability to successfully recruit, train and manage *at the scale* necessary to feed the revenue expectations of your company. Your talent pipeline is the far end of the revenue generation machine and should be managed like it.

Hiring the right players is the most important job you have.

Part 1: Hire Only A-Players
Part 2: The Tech Sales MBA
Part 3: The Interview Funnel
Part 4: Interviewing in Execution
Part 5: Roundtabling
Part 6: Closing Candidates
Part 7: Group Interviewing

Part 1: Hire Only A-Players

"Someone who is exceptional in their role is not just a little better than someone who is pretty good. They are 100 times better." - Mark Zuckerberg

Our perception on the impact of A-Players vs. everyone else is skewed.

A-players need less management, perform at excellence and drive others to become better. Not only do they crush quota, but they help every SDR, including future SDRs, to do so as well. They raise the bar - and in some cases will push you to become better yourself.

They are the 10x (or 100x) impact.

Hiring **only** A-players is especially important early in the development of your Sales Development team, when it has yet to reach optimal efficiency. In the high-leverage, early-development stages, the impact of a single SDR can be enormous. They will set the tone and culture for years to come.

SDR organizations I run have had acceptance rates as low as 4% from application. That's a significantly lower chance than getting into Harvard (5.9%), Wharton (9%) or Cal-Berkley (18%) - and many of the SDRs applying come those schools.

Have the courage and self-confidence to hire people more talented than everyone else in the room (including you). That confidence crafts the future of a great team and brings in 100x players.

Talent over Capacity
Resist the urge to hire in order to have the capacity available to hit your goals. One of the biggest mistakes with hiring is the need to take candidates simply to fill headcount - settling for mediocrity because they will fill quota.

Do not do this.

It is long-term pain, a Band-Aid that will become infected - someone who performs at slightly less than average becomes a drag on the future of your entire team.

Go High-Beta

Instead, take candidates who are high-risk (high-beta) over those you know are average. These candidates could be great or might flame out, but at least you'll know quickly.

The trick with these candidates, once they turn into employees, is to have active management ramping them whilst evaluating if they are a fit. This requires strong management, leadership and a robust training program (explored in Part II).

You should prefer to find out if someone is not a fit, and manage out, rather than miss on a game-changing SDR that could lead the future of your organization.

Known mediocre players will also be a drain on your leadership team and your high-performers. Just to get to quota they will take the time of everyone around them. Avoid at all costs.

Trajectory over Experience

A-players will pull your organization forward through the brilliance of their trajectory alone. They will be excited about the impact they can have on your team more than the accomplishments they have already created.

I can remember one specific example when interviewing Tracy, a SDR who would later be promoted to manager within a year. Not only did her resume show an increasing trajectory of responsibilities and achievements, but she demonstrated how she would add value *during her interview* by bringing a slew of email templates she had written on behalf of our team. You could see the trajectory already making a difference.

Candidates resting on the laurels of their former accomplishments - who have been in SDR positions for years - may fit in with your organization when growth goals are less ambitious. But while you're building a high-octane, growth start-up you don't have the luxury of even one player getting complacent, burning out, infecting others or bringing down the level of play. Even all-time great teams will sometimes play down to the level of the competition. Don't let this be an option.

While you are trying to grow 10x, you need only high-trajectory 100x players.

GSD vs. Story Tellers

People who Get Shit Done always do. They find a way and they don't make drama about it. GSD candidates focus on their impact and the results.

On the other hand, Story Tellers weave intricate and elaborate stories about how difficult a task was to achieve. They focus on the challenges and environmental factors.

To weed out Story Tellers, get people to perform exercises during the interview process. We'll discuss role-play and email exercise later, but these are critical to assessing whether you have someone who will roll their sleeves up and GSD or someone who is good at selling themselves.

GSD candidates are challenged by and enjoy a rigorous interview process. Story Tellers will self-select out.

Greatness is Consistency

Lastly, do not hire job hoppers unless they have a very compelling story (i.e. went to Africa for 6 months to start a NGO).

Generally, candidates who jump from job to job every year have not performed well enough for their companies to make the extra effort to keep them or they have been poorly qualifying one of the most important decisions of their lives -- where they work. Either way, it's not good.

Excellence is defined by **consistently** delivering high-performance. LeBron James personifies excellence because he *averages* 28 points per game over the 13+ years of his career so far. A-players perform at a high level year in, year out; they excelled during their time in high school, at university and on the job.

Although not always a strict disqualification, job hoppers require extra attention.

Part 2: The Tech Sales MBA

SDR talent is the extreme front-end of the company's revenue pipeline. In order to give it more structure, it is important to be able to recruit All-Star talent **at scale and predictably**. To do so, you must commit to a talent value proposition. My commitment to each candidate is a Tech Sales MBA.

As millennials enter the workforce, the expectations around careers have changed. The demand from this generation is for structure and stability. As most of the young professionals have born witness (or the brunt) of the Great Recession, structure and stability reassures them in an uncertain time. The clearer a picture and vision you can paint, the more attractive the position.

When speaking about professional development it's no longer enough to tell this generation to "do a good job" and they'll be taken care of. In the age of Snapchat and Candy Crush, their expectations are that they will receive continual feedback and work within a well-defined structure to progress their careers. This is not too dissimilar to other professions like banking or law, where there are industry-standard expectations on progression. Sales Development suffers from a lack of vision on the same type of system, leading to an inability to recruit at scale.

Companies should develop the SDR role as a Tech Sales MBA; 2-3 years of hands-on and classroom style learning about sales and entrepreneurship. Should SDRs succeed, this will culminate in the opportunity to interview for a highly lucrative position in the field or wherever their passion may lead them. All the while they get to learn the skills on how to run and scale a company from the inside out. A springboard to a successful career in technology, that is what Sales Development sells and delivers to our talent. Using this bridge from college to the professional world speaks directly to the need for structure in the language of the millennial and properly guides expectations for everyone.

Additionally, the enterprise technology sales role is ripe for disruption by young talent. As more of our nation's talent turns away from careers in stodgy finance, private equity or law, they will be looking for highly lucrative jobs where they know they are providing real value. An older generation that fell into enterprise tech sales will be replaced by the best of one which will choose enterprise tech sales.

Sales Development leaders must then uphold the Tech Sales MBA vision by delivering on opportunities to learn about sales, entrepreneurship and the technology industry for those SDRs exceeding expectations (and, of course, quota). The street works both ways - if we expect millennials to grind hard, we need to build the infrastructure, transparency and feedback that will get them a Tech Sales MBA.

Part 3: The Interview Funnel

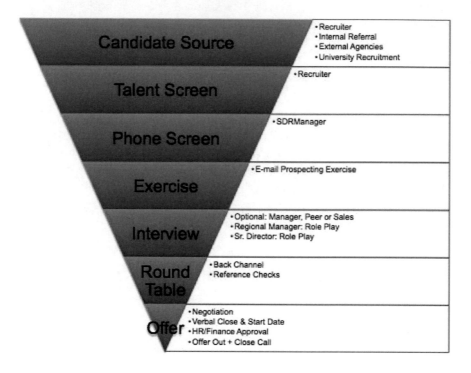

The interview process is a funnel just like the sales funnel. It begins with resumes and ends with closed candidates. Optimizing the funnel and conversion is a direct analogy to executing across the sales pipeline. It is, however, a role reversal. In this case the Talent organization are the SDRs and SDR leaders get to close.

The first part of the funnel to optimize is sourcing candidates. Set qualification criteria around your ideal target profile (ITP) and get as specific as possible. Sit down with your recruiter to analyze and evaluate resumes together. Review and analyze the resumes of your current team to find out what has worked, and what hasn't.

Monitor conversion rates at every step to understand where there may be weakness in the pipeline. Regularly (weekly) review the pipeline and candidate forecast with your managers and talent team. If you treat it like a sales pipeline, you will soon see it produce like one.

Side Note: Exercise Caution with Agencies

Generally, working with external recruitment agencies will be a pain unless you have the cycles to actively manage the relationship. Incentives don't align - they are often shopping a single candidate to multiple highly-divergent companies. This can make the process confusing and result in a poorly prepared candidate or a bad candidate experience.

These relationships can be workable, but you will need to set aside time to keep agencies honest and productive. The extended interview cycle necessary to attract and vet A+ players doesn't work well for agencies who won't or can't afford to wait.

It is most productive to ask your own managers and SDRs to source candidates themselves. Prospecting is their core job, after all! You can manage this in a similar fashion as to any sales SPIFF or competition.

Lastly, university recruitment should be a much larger feeder for the sales development community. The jobs exist, but the relationship and market awareness within the university network does not. Ask Alumni on your team to reach back out to their networks. Look for on-campus groups with interests that align with your company and stage recruitment events. Entrepreneurship groups can be a great source of talent for early stage companies.

Some markets, like London, are especially difficult to recruit from. Generally, tech hasn't matured as a viable industry and sales is not looked at as a place to start a career. It is here where working with on-campus entrepreneurial groups can be particularly valuable, as these students are actively interested in growth companies and open to new career trajectories. The same opportunity exists for universities outside of the Bay Area in the United States, most notably the mid-west and south.

Part 4: Interviewing in Execution

Interviewing should be viewed as having 4 distinct goals.

1. Gather *data* about a candidate's achievements
2. Evaluate the candidate's ability to perform in role and to take coaching
3. Understand what motivates the candidate and if that fits a sales career at your company
4. Communicate to the candidate the vision/values for the company and team

Goal #1: Data Points of Excellence

In order to find excellence, a candidate must able to produce top-tier results against their peers. Remember that greatness is consistent excellence, so you should be able to find plenty of examples over the course of the life of a great candidate.

Past performance is indicative of future performance.

There's plenty to work with, even in new graduates. Here's a typical answer from a new undergraduate, Edan, when asked about his education:

> "In college I majored in business and accounting at ASU. I was really drawn to business because my father studied it. In my freshman year I joined a fraternity and eventually became rush chair president. Later, during my sophomore year I joined the Ultimate Frisbee Club and became president of that club. It was a lot of fun and I really became a leader in that group."

Sounds like a decent answer - this Sun Devil was active and involved. What's the problem here?

Well, it's a typical answer which details responsibilities -- but nothing about the results. There's no **data** with which to compare Edan against his peers or context to evaluate how impressive his accomplishments actually are. Let's see what happens when Edan revises his answer:

> "I joined ASU to major in business because the W.P. Carey School of Business ranked in the top 5 in accounting, which I majored in following the footsteps of my dad. I graduated with a cumulative 3.7 and major 3.75 GPA, summa cum laude - top 15% of my class.
>
> During my freshman year, I joined one of the most prestigious fraternities on campus, SAE, and became rush chair president after a competitive election against 5 other brothers. Elected on the promise of better organization, we recruited a class that was 150% larger than the year before. Our ability to prepare in the summer and our engagement in freshman orientation activities made the biggest difference.
>
> I wanted to explore something physically active my sophomore year, so I decided to join Ultimate Frisbee and I really found a passion. As senior captain of the team, I instituted more accountability - resulting in a few more practices each month and 4 more wins than the year before I was captain. It was really enjoyable to form a great bond and have a positive impact on the team."

Notice how in the second answer Edan was able to produce both results **and** the specific tactics that got him there. This shows not only the ability to deliver excellence, but the self-awareness to understand why he was successful. The ability to do this will serve Edan well moving forward as he seeks to continually improve his sales process and methodology.

It is your job as the interviewer to tease these data points of excellence from a candidate. Not all interviewees will approach the interview from this perspective naturally. You may need to coach candidates and ask clarifying questions.

I've interviewed over 500 SDR candidates (and counting), hiring over 100 while losing only a handful to bad performance. The strategy used is basic, but effective; I tell them exactly how I am looking for them to answer a question, ask them a question and evaluate if they have delivered based on the criteria I gave them.

Interview Set-up

"Thanks for coming in today. I appreciate you making the time and (build rapport)...

Well, here we only hire A-players who have an increasing trajectory of accomplishments - we believe these folks who crush it before will continue to do so here. After all, past performance is a good indicator of future performance, so that's what we're looking for. Since we focus on results and metrics, we call what we are looking for "data points of excellence".

So, first, I'd like for you to drive me through your work and education history while focusing on your data points of excellence. I am also looking for you to provide context.

For instance, let's say I wanted to talk about your time as captain of your school's championship soccer team. I'd like to know how you were elected captain, what division your team played in, how many wins you had and what you did differently than the captains of the past to increase those wins.

This is not the time to be humble; I'm looking for the best you! It's a sales job, so remember to sell yourself. Sound good? Let's start."

The point of the interview is to bring the best out of each candidate - not to trick them.

Once you've collected the data behind their achievements, you can compare that to other members of your existing team and ask yourself if the candidate's results and trajectory would likely raise the bar for the members already on the squad.

In this way you can incrementally, but steadily, raise the level of excellence.

Goal #2: Evaluate the candidate's ability to perform in role and to take coaching

At the very minimum, use two role-plays and an email writing exercise during your interview process.

These are the two main methods to interact with prospects. You want to make sure candidates are naturally comfortable or skilled at both. Since you will be providing feedback, these exercises will evaluate both their ability to execute and to be coachable.

Role-Play Set-Up

"Alright, so let's get down to the fun part, the Role Play. You should have received an email with the criteria we use to grade role plays, so I hope you're prepared. The purpose of the Role Play is to put you in the seat of being an SDR, like we hired you today.

So, let's say we hired you on the spot and put you on the account team for McDonald's. McDonald's has been having issues with their international growth, specifically China, and has had stagnant revenue the last few quarters.

Let's say I am the CIO of McDonald's and you are a newly-minted SDR for our company. The purpose of your call is to secure a 30 minute meeting with me and your AE. Are you ready now, or would you like a minute to prepare before we start?"

Most good candidates take the minute to ask clarifying questions, build a PPOV, or link the customer case studies they've researched. Less qualified candidates will immediately start in on their elevator pitch, without customizing for the account or prospect role.

By choosing McDonald's in this scenario (or any account consistently), you can compare candidate answers across interviews.

Especially for the role-play, give your evaluation criteria to the candidate *before* interviews. Since many candidates do not have any sales or professional experience they need a framework within which to prepare.

Once they execute on their first role-play, give them feedback on their performance and have a different interviewer run another role-play. The difference in performance will give you an indication on their ability to learn, take feedback and dynamically improve. In essence, are they coachable?

Top criteria to look for in a role-play exercise and that are shared with candidates prior to their interview:

- **Strength of Introduction:** Candidates should ask for time and demonstrate value early on.
- **Use of Customer Voice**: Use of your company's case studies and success stories.
- **Understanding of Company and Positioning**: Do they understand what you do and craft a point of view on how that impacts a prospect?
- **Qualification of Need / Open Questioning:** Obtained or tried to obtain enough information to gain a good understanding of prospect's need by using open questions.
- **Objection Handling**: Ability to handle obstacles like questions on pricing or competitors in a thoughtful and skillful manner. They should be able to direct the conversation back to their own agenda.
- **Presumptive Close:** Presumptive and effective close that clearly outlines the next appropriate action.
- **Active Listening**: Does the candidate listen using affirmative verbal cues and rephrases what is said in a thoughtful manner?
- **Tenacity**: Does the candidate deal well with adversity and continue to pursue his/her goals on the call no matter what?

Email Exercise

Beyond the Role Play, candidates should be assessed on their ability to write effectively and professionally. Prospect expectations on communication have shifted with the evolution of the cell phone - more communication is being done electronically via email, text or social media than ever before.

Now, most of the value provided to prospects need to be delivered via those electronic channels. This makes the ability to write in clear and concise language one of the most important skills for an SDR to have. A great SDR no longer has to have a silver tongue, but a rapier for a pen.

The email exercise should also test a candidate's ability to develop a Provocative Point of View (PPOV) about an account and simulate an email exchange with a prospect, including common objections.

This will give you insight into a candidate's ability to respond in a "live-fire" exercise. Using a Google Survey works well for this.

Top Criteria to look for in the Email Exercise:
- **Content Accuracy**: Does the email deliver content true to your company? Candidate should be able to distill content/messaging from your website/interviews and represent it correctly.
- **Well-researched with PPOV:** Does the email demonstrate the candidate's ability to find and effectively message around relevant information about the prospect?
- **Concise**: Does the email deliver value economically? Candidate should not use filler words.
- **Articulate**: Does the email deliver valuable content clearly? Candidates should choose to use simpler words over complex ones.
- **Correct Grammar**: Does the email use correct English? Candidate should be able to use English effectively and structure their email to flow in a conversational and logical manner.
- **Call to Action**: Is there a clear call to action in the email?

Part 5: Roundtabling

Once all the interviews have taken place and the prospecting activity is completed, a roundtable should be held between interviewers to assess the candidate's performance and compare findings. It is vital to make decisions in this method to avoid the "gut-feel" decision-making too often employed in hiring.

The goal of the roundtable meeting is to collect information on the candidate, explore each interviewer's experience and opinions, dive deeply into any concerns and, if moving forward, to agree on a close plan.

Roundtables also keep the management team accountable to hiring to the company's core values. Although the hiring manager should own the end-decision, this visibility and accountability of the roundtable forces her to do her homework and think through the hire.

A Candidate Assessment Form makes up the basis of analysis and discussion during the roundtable. The Candidate Assessment Form should be a collaborative document where interviewers can share their notes and a hire/no-hire grade. These should be all filled out prior to the roundtable for group review, but the hire/no-hire grade should be hidden until the end to prevent groupthink.

The most important part of the roundtable for hiring managers to understand is that they are *not* on the hook for justifying the hiring of a candidate. Rather, their role is to facilitate a conversation that best explores a candidate's qualification. A successful roundtable can result in a no-hire decision.

A good roundtable simply seeks to understand the most about the candidate's data points of excellence, performance during exercises, motivations and buy-in into the company's vision. With this information, then the hiring manager can make an informed decision.

In general, reference checks should be done **before** roundtable to give the group as much information as possible in the final assessment of the candidate. However, reference checks should only be used to confirm facts the candidate has presented herself. Since most reference checks are biased towards or coached by the candidate, they almost never tell a negative story (so take even small hesitations seriously). If possible, a careful back-channel check before roundtable is the most valuable thing you can do to gain insight on a candidate.

Preparation is key to a great roundtable. It is important the entire interview panel reads the notes in the assessment form in advance and understands the strengths and weaknesses of the candidate. That way you're not rehashing basic facts about the candidate, like his quota performance. Everyone should know that the candidate achieved 156% of quota last year.

Rather, if quota is an area of concern, the conversation should revolve around an exploration of the context of the candidate's performance. The fact that the 156% quota was based on closed-won business and that is was all sourced from a single deal makes it much less compelling.

In roundtables the hiring manager should present what she's learned about the candidate and then explore the areas of concern with the interview team.

Part 6: Closing Candidates

Given the amount of time and investment made to get candidates through the interview process, it is essential to close candidates quickly and effectively. Getting them on-board quickly avoids losing them to alternative offers and keeps the positive momentum rolling into their employment as an SDR.

If the roundtable is positive and a decision to hire is made, end with leaving the roundtable with a clear plan to close the candidate leveraging the wider team.

Close plans should include:
- Expressing why the team selected and is excited about the candidate
- Communicating a vision of the candidate's career with the company
- Explanation of the Compensation, Commission and Benefits
- Verbal close on offer acceptance and start date

Hiring managers should also use dinners, social events or executive outreach to close candidates. Executive outreach should align with a candidate's career interest. So, for instance, if a candidate expresses interest in Marketing, then the CMO should be introduced to the candidate during the interview or close process. Not only does this set the stage for a potential path later, it also shows the intentionality around professional development that millennials crave.

A dinner, lunch or other social event is mandatory for every hire I make. For young professionals, these extra-curricular events can be of vital importance. Outside of the interview room you can gauge how they interact with others and to see how they fit within the culture of the team. In informal settings it is also easier for candidates to open up about their passions and motivations. Lastly, introducing them to successful team members at a social event will help candidates visualize their own success and impact.

Part 7: Group Interviewing

Interviewing in ones and twos, however, may not be enough if you are looking to grow an SDR organization quickly. A detailed interview process can take a hiring manager 5 hours or more per candidate. Screening, Interviewing, Roundtabling, Exercises, Back channels, References and Notes each take a chunk from a hiring manager's day.

For myself, it has been necessary to hire as many as 5+ new SDRs each month across a global team; ambitious growth goals and promotion attrition drove the need to hire. Group interviewing proved to be the solution to hire at scale.

A half or full-day group interview will be your best bet. This will allow you to evaluate entire classes of candidates in one go; typically between 10 to 20 at a time.

Much like an SDR recruiting attendees for an event, have your talent team recruit for a Group Interview Assessment Day. Depending on your budget and bar for talent, you can choose to stay local or arrange travel for some candidates as well.

The magic with group interviews is that it is much easier to spot top-tier talent. The group will naturally select and feature the most talented and/or alpha candidates.

The assessment days I ran spanned 6 hours and typically resulted in 2-3 hires per class, or 5-10% conversion. The day ran in four parts: Introductions, Team Exercises, Presentations and Individual Interviews.

Group Interviewing: Introductions

The first introduction to make is your company's introduction to the candidates. It is important to have your pitch down and to be able to present a truthful and compelling vision for your SDR organization and the Tech Sales MBA.

The focus should be on the core values that the company holds, the benefits the company can bring to the candidate's professional career and the high expectations leadership expects from any candidate hired. This last point, particularly, will get candidates fired up about the highly competitive group interview process to come.

Once the company, team and management have been introduced it is time for the candidates to introduce themselves to the group. Typically, asking them to present their Most Significant Achievement (MSA) sets the right tone of excellence and competition.

In the confidence, logic and articulation shown in introducing themselves, it is often possible to determine the wheat from the chaff. Keep notes on each candidate in a collaborative document so that the evaluation team can reference later -- faces can get confused when evaluating so many candidates at one time.

Group Interview: Team Exercises

The next stage of group interviewing should put the candidates through a team exercise. Understanding how candidates work in a team setting helps you to evaluate how they would interact within the very competitive, but collaborative world that is Sales Development. Candidates also typically self-select leaders very naturally, making the vetting process easier on you.

Split the group up into teams of 8-10 and choose a team building exercise with a well-defined goal. Instruct them to choose a leader to present their findings at the end.

During the exercise usually 1-2 candidates rise to the top and coordinate the others. Additionally, you can evaluate the logic of each of the candidates and whether they listen carefully to instructions.

Group Interview: Presentations and Exercise

After the team exercises it's time to get to know the candidates individually. Presentations on why sales and why they want to work for your company can be helpful in both evaluating the candidate and ensuring that they think through why they are interviewing for the job in the first place.

Elite talent have plenty of options in the job market and so it's important to ensure that they've spent some time thinking about why they're interested - it's a great qualifying exercise for both parties involved.

With presentations, just like every other part of the interview process, it is important to know what qualities you are looking for. Brainstorm with your team success criteria, and be sure to share that with the candidates themselves before the day of the interview so they have time to prepare.

While each candidate presents to the hiring panel, it is optimal to have the other candidates work on the email exercise to maximize the number of data points collected and to keep the candidates engaged.

Group Interview: Individual Interviews
Once you've seen the presentations, it's time to narrow the field to only those who you want to interview. This usually results in a 50-75% drop-off from the main group - depending on how well your recruiter qualified.

Since you've been with the candidates all day, you can get away with shorter 30 minute interviews. There should be at least 3 interviewers and each should focus on picking up a specific topic: data points of excellence, career/motivation and role-play.

Once individual interviews are complete, the team should release the individual interview candidates to a social event with the team and complete roundtables while that is going on. With so many candidates, it is difficult to keep track of your thoughts on them even 48 hours later so roundtabling immediately will result in the best evaluation.

Caveat! Group interviewing works well when the SDR model is proven and you have reached a state in the business where further investment in the group will yield predictable results. It is best to have already built a rigorous on-boarding program before beginning to group interview and ingesting new SDRs at scale.

You should always hire in classes by grouping start dates together to reduce training load, but should only group interview when you have a predictable training process in place.

Chapter 5
TRAINING CHAMPIONS

Training is critical to SDR success because it sets them on the trajectory for their career. Once they start to execute, it is a lot harder for them to learn. The hamster wheel of quota is real and the habits SDRs pick up early will inform their performance down the line.

Does your on-boarding process consist of new hires sitting next to the highest performer in your group? "Training by osmosis" seems to be a great way to give All-star reps more responsibility and get new SDRs up and running.

Unfortunately, this type of training has neither the rigor, scalability nor accountability that is necessary to enable young professionals to be successful.

A slightly evolved system might start with an excel checklist and a playbook filled with Salesforce screenshots. Now, this might be a little better (I guess?) but it still lacks real rigor around learning.

Instead, maybe we should try to bring in consultants that specialize in sales training - surely that will be a quick fix?

Sorry, this does not work either - *there are no quick fixes.*

Because the consultants and their methodology are gone in the next week, there's no way to reinforce, test or certify your SDRs on the knowledge they were just taught. As soon as their consultants are gone, no one credible will be there to hold them accountable to it.

Effective Sales Development leaders must be able to teach Sales Development best practices and tactics themselves.

How credible is a leader who cannot coach his own team? Does five-time NBA champion Coach Gregg Popovich outsource training and coaching? No, he does not. If you don't have an understanding of the core fundamentals, then you are not providing enough value to your team. As a leader it is not your job to execute on the play - Pop doesn't take many jumpers or lift many weights anymore - but he has to be able to understand and coach to the fundamentals.

Consultants also don't know your business like you do, and they lack the ability to effectively create company specific takeaways with credibility. Making sure that the lessons are *specific* is essential with new grads who need prescriptive guidance.

Beyond the skills for the job, Sales Development leaders have the responsibility to bring new talent into the workforce, to teach them the central tenants of becoming a professional.

This chapter explores the core fundamentals that fresh graduates need to master and the importance of building an on-boarding experience that parallels the rigor of classroom style learning. Lastly, it will cover the need for a robust playbook that is a living document that defines your team.

Part 1: The Fundamentals
Part 2: The Perfect Trainer
Part 3: The SDR Syllabus
Part 4: The Certification
Part 5: The SDR Playbook

Part 1: The Fundamentals

We often take for granted the basics we've learned over the years. Educating young talent on what is expected of them every day and *why* they should be doing it is critical to their success. These are fundamentals upon which your house is built.

PCS is a basic framework I've distilled to consistently reinforce the core values individual SDRs need to master in order to become productive professionals.

PCS: Preparation, Concentration and Separation

Preparation - "By failing to prepare, you are preparing to fail." - Benjamin Franklin

- **Plan Ahead of Time**: Aim to maximize the value of every interaction with thoughtful and thorough preparation. If you don't think it's going to be valuable, don't do it (cancel the meeting). Make sure you've allocated enough time during or before your meetings to get all of your deliverables done within the allotted time frame. In this way you should never be late to meetings, have meetings overrun or miss deadlines.
- **Practice is Not Enough**: Get to excellence. Only *perfect practice makes perfect*. Do your core process until you are perfect. Then do it one more time to make sure you're consistent.
- **Put in the hours:** Those who came before you have, those competing against you certainly are and our competitors aren't going to hand us anything. And in a company full of intelligent A-players, the first differentiator is going to be hard work.
- **Preparation creates Stability:** Most "emergency" meetings or situations would have never happened if there had been the proper planning, process and execution. Create the ability to give yourself stability through preparation. Stability gives you unimpeded time to concentrate (see next bullet) and space for separation (see last bullet). **For this**

reason, preparation is the most important fundamental to master.

Concentration - Every work day is game day, every process a play ran.

- **Train Your Mind**: Mental concentration or "flow" is a muscle that can be trained - challenge yourself to extend the length and intensity with which you can execute every day. The length at which you can be in a mental workflow uninterrupted is what you should consider your work day (i.e. it's not just about sitting in a chair looking busy).
- **Destroy Distractions**: Do not interrupt your concentration flow because you lose efficiency getting out of and back into flow. Turn off Skype/IM/TXT notifications or be disciplined not to check. Block time for personal tasks (texts, reading news articles, grocery lists etc.) to leave workflow unhindered while still taking care of yourself. Try to keep your flow for an hour or more at a time to get to efficiency.
- **Put Your Game Face On**: Did your prospect just sit down at her desk? Clock's running. Got a connect? Run the right sales play. Did you get a W today? Good - tomorrow you get a chance for another one. Every day is game day - so put your game face on when the clock starts.

Separation - All execution and no vision makes Jack a lost boy.

- **Keep Work from Creeping**: Once you have achieved a state where you can exercise an intense productive flow throughout the course of the day…keep it contained. Constantly thinking about work (or any one topic) will lead to stagnation because there is no space for creativity. Be entirely present where you are during your free-time and weekends to rejuvenate yourself.
- **Take Balcony Time**: Regularly think, reflect and organize your broader thoughts. Apply these to your plan and vision for yourself, your team, the SDR group and the company - and you should have a vision for each of these. Personally, I use Sunday nights. The reason "shower thoughts" can be

so powerful are that they come at a time where you give yourself freedom to think creatively. Knowing where you are going and why you are going there will also make you more confident in your daily execution.

Young professionals straight from college are used to procrastinating until midterms, delivering papers only when they are due and executing in a highly-structured environment. Their time had been managed for them. The scope and quality of work they produce has always been decided by someone else (a teacher) and rigorously monitored.

Unfortunately, as we know, that's not how the professional world works. Typically, it is just the results which are monitored, maybe some of the process and definitely not someone's time. Give millennials clear guidelines and expectations on how to conduct themselves. And reinforce it often.

Part 2: The Perfect Trainer

In building the bridge from university and their professional career, instituting a highly accountable classroom experience helps to settle young professionals down comfortably. This is a familiar concept to millennials and one in which, if you've done your interviewing correctly, they have been thriving in.

Delivering a classroom experience begins with constructing a mission for your onboarding program. The mission my team and I developed for our onboarding program was:

> "The SDR training program uses daily exercises and real-time feedback to build confidence in sales skills and messaging. Delivered in less than 4 weeks, our mission is to establish the foundation to mastery of the SDR role as quickly as possible."

One of our SDR managers at MuleSoft, Amanda, has a clear passion for training and onboarding. She had the responsibility of running our global training program that consistently ramped high-performing quota crushing SDRs in two months. Amanda not only developed the training program, but held the other managers accountable to delivering it with excellence.

This is how she would challenge us all to be better coaches and trainers:

THE PERFECT TRAINER

•**The perfect trainer is patient.** She has the emotional intelligence to anticipate what concepts will take more time to digest than others. She explains sales and product related concepts with clarity, but not assuming that everything will be easily understood. She allows time for the trainee to digest the material. She realizes that each trainee is different, and will therefore learn differently. She creates a culture of trust and openness where curiosity is encouraged. She is honest with her feedback, and while friendly, not a friend – priority #1 is getting the SDR trained and ramped, and she will do what it takes to make sure that they are.

•**The perfect trainer is intentional.** She is 100% dedicated to enabling the new SDR in all enablement sessions, and is present to nothing else. She runs training sessions that include nothing but training related material. She does not check her phone, email, or Skype unless it is pertinent to the enablement subject matter at hand. She is prepared for all 1:1s with data-driven analyses, and follows through with related "in-the-trenches" attack plans. The perfect trainer is committed to the outcome of the perfect SDR.

•**The perfect trainer is accountable.** She delivers on her promises. She does what she says. She shows up for all sessions on time. She can be relied on as the go-to-resource for anything the trainee needs. She establishes a relationship of trust, respect, and dependability. In turn, she holds her trainees accountable to developing knowledge on messaging, positioning and SDR process. She holds her trainees accountable to using all of their faculties in preparing for and concentrating on learning. Lastly, she holds herself and the trainee accountable for the new SDR's morale and confidence.

•**The perfect trainer is consistent.** She not only delivers on her promises but ALWAYS delivers on her promises. She starts every day with "Framing the Day," and finishes every day with reviewing her trainee's work/progress. She consistently demonstrates patience, intentionality, and accountability. You can always rely on the perfect trainer.

Part 3: The SDR Syllabus

New graduates need the structure of a syllabus to guide their learning. As Amanda mentions in her description of a perfect trainer, for each day of training new reps and their managers need to have a set of goals.

Trainers and trainees should review these at the beginning of the day and meet at the end of the day to reinforce this knowledge. During the end of day check, managers should ask the reps to demonstrate or practice what they learned.

While each day has specific learning goals, the method of doing so should not always be prescribed to the trainees. Instead, make resources and options to learn available to them.

For instance, if one day's topic is "Learn how to open a call", list several activities and resources available to trainees:

1. Read a call guide with examples and best practices
2. Listen to pre-recorded calls
3. Listen to live calls with other SDRs
4. Practice role play with manager and/or SDR Buddy
5. Call C-grade leads with live prospects

Since each SDR learns differently - visually, through practice or through observation - let the SDRs themselves determine how they want to learn. The important part is that trainees know that at the end of the day they will be held accountable to the goal set out at the beginning of the day.

Now, you might think that such hands-on training may be a lot of work, especially when training only 1 or 2 SDRs at a time...Yes, it is! But that is the work that matters and the secret to getting consistent performance out of your SDRs as soon as possible.

A challenging and hands-on training program also harnesses the enthusiasm of new reps and leverages them when they are most open to learning. Pointing them toward a high-upward trajectory early on will set them on a path toward success.

Great managers need to be able to get their hands dirty to help their SDRs early and often. The hard work we put into evaluating and signing talent doesn't end until 2-3 years later when SDRs are ready for their next role.

That means getting into the weeds from day one.

Part 4: The Certification

The culmination of training should result in certification to reinforce learning. I suggest certification come in three parts: exam, role play and presentation.

Trainees usually take certification very seriously and will do well; since it holds them highly accountable in a "finals" format, they understand the gravity of certification.

During each part of certification, nominate a panel of managers, team leaders or veteran SDRs to grade what the trainee did well and what he could improve on. Share this feedback verbally in real-time and send it to the trainee later as a document as well.

Any trainees which failed to pass certification should receive extra coaching and another chance when they were ready. A failure at certification is a very big red flag. It is both an early opportunity to coach and to evaluate if the SDR continues to be the right fit. Remember that our strategy during hiring in Part I was to hire high-beta candidates, and certification can help to determine if they are working out very quickly. However, if you set clear expectations and examples of "A-level" performance during training, failure at certification will very rarely happen.

After the SDR certifies, then they should start carrying quota. It is important not to swamp them with actual quota before they are certified so they have enough space to learn without the pressure of hitting a number. If you give them quota or accounts too early they will start to do "real" work and lock-in bad habits before you get a chance to fix them. That is not to say that they shouldn't be making calls or writing sending emails during training, they should be. SDR in training just shouldn't own a number.

Training works like an elevator - wherever they stop is usually where they stay - so it's important to invest the time early for long-term success.

Certification: Exam

An exam should test company messaging, product knowledge and positioning. The goal of the test is to force SDRs to become the experts on your product and to be able to communicate the value of your solution in detail. This should give them the confidence to be able to provide value to prospects who probably have 15-20 years in the industry.

For companies who are looking to sell into the enterprise space, our prospects typically are sophisticated and highly knowledgeable CIOs or heads of business. It can be hard for new SDRs to have the confidence to speak directly with these executives without some sort of comparative advantage.

That advantage has to come from the knowledge of your company's product, customer case studies and deployment ROI in detail. In this way, the value they bring will be to match the customer's environment and strategic goals to what the product can do and the results that drives.

The foundation of this knowledge should be built, reinforced and tested through a written exam in order to get to depth of knowledge necessary to challenge a prospect's current method of doing business.

Certification: Role Play

Use role-play certification to ensure that the SDR can apply that depth of knowledge in real-time. The more robust the role play scenario, the better to simulate real-life.

To simulate a complex call environment, my SDRs get in a conference room with an assessment panel and make mock calls to several different managers or veterans. A prompt prepares each actor to play a different role within an account that the trainee SDR will own.

Each call will be to different prospect profiles in order to test the trainee on different topics (i.e. objection handling, competitive positioning, cold/unwilling etc.). Optimally, each actor would be simulating a real person in the account.

Role-play can be the most nerve wracking part of certification because it is in-role, live action and evaluated by peers. The actors also know all the SDR plays and company product positioning, so they can be much tougher than regular prospects. However, if your SDR can crush the mock call in this environment, you can be confident she's ready to perform well when in front of a prospect. And her confidence is what really matters.

Certification: Presentation
The last part of certification is a presentation on account penetration. The goal of this presentation is to evaluate the trainee's ability to strategically approach his territory.

Typically, I have trainees select 5 accounts in their territory and stack rank them -- explaining why and the criteria they used to evaluate.

For the top 2, they need demonstrate how they will prospect into the account, who they are targeting, and the cadence they were using to engage their prospect (cadence strategy discussed in Part IV).

The most valuable portion would then be to do a deep dive into their prospecting cadence, specifically reviewing the content of their email templates and LinkedIn messages.

This is the culmination of their certification, as it shows how well they have internalized what they learned in the written exam and puts their ability to make calls into the broader context of the cadences they will execute.

Part 5: The SDR Playbook

If you don't have a playbook, you need one. Your team and especially your trainees need one. A playbook should be a living document that forms the foundational values guiding your team, your core IP and the rules that govern play. It is especially important for global, high-growth or decentralized teams.

The playbook is a reference document which any SDR can go to in order to understand their roles, responsibilities, Service Level Agreements (SLAs) and common definitions. It ensures that there is one common language, framework, methodology and philosophy.

Many times, best practices and tactics crept into my playbooks - those should be housed in a separate area where SDRs can go that is specific to training and skilling. Instead, think of the playbook as a document that a new hire could use to understand what the SDR role entails and how the group runs -- but not the specifics on what or how to do their day-to-day job.

The Playbook covers:
- Core Values
- Team Structure
- Roles and Responsibilities
- Lead Ownership Rules
- Account Ownership Rules
- SAL & Qualification Definition
- Tooling Definition
- Activity Definition
- Lead Status Definition
- Hand-Off Process
- Compensation
- Out of Office Policy

Much of the playbook should be specific to your team, company, market, technology and organizational design. It is important, however, to document your decisions and definitions in one place to ensure consistency.

I *always* have a Google Doc of the playbook open and am making comments/revisions on a day-to-day basis in an unpublished "Editor's Edition". One member of my leadership team owns the playbook as its editor to ensure all the changes fit together and that they are documented. From there, we'll review and approve changes once a month. When there has been substantial change, it is time to publish the next version out to the team and quiz them on it to ensure it has been internalized.

Like your business, your playbook should be constantly evolving to best match the realities of the market. Playbooks often lose value because of the fast-paced and dynamic evolution of technology. Institute rigor around its development to avoid stagnation.

Chapter 6
Coaching Millennials

This chapter discusses motivating a millennial SDR team. Specifically it will cover the core values around the Manager-SDR relationship, how to ensure your coaches are on top of their game and the evolving concept of Agile Professional Development.

One of the biggest difficulties in managing them SDRs is managing their expectations. Early on in a career, it is easy for young workers to feel like everything is exaggerated - and indeed it is, because it is the first time they are experiencing many of these things!

The first time you broke up with your girl/boyfriend, got stung by a bee or heard Adele sing were probably highly impactful moments. Now, after you've put Adele on every one of your Spotify playlists and have heard her everyday on the radio, your reaction is probably tempered. Similarly, young professionals will often "over"react to any stimulus. SDR leaders need to have the patience and experience to teach SDRs about professional patience by providing context.

Furthermore, millennials desire to understand how their work impacts others and how that fits into their passions. Jobs are no longer a means to an end. They are the passions and lives of young professionals. Managers need to get to know each SDRs individually, to understand how they are motivated and what they are motivated by.

By providing context and linking to impact, Sales Development can help to bring a new generation of professionals into the fold.

Part 1: Provide Context and Link to Impact
Part 2: Motivate the Individual
Part 3: The Team Contract
Part 4: Coach the Coaches
Part 5: Agile Professional Development

Part 1: Provide Context and Link to Impact

Young workers are passionate about making an impact. Tap into that by providing context on how their success ties in with the company's goals.

The SDR role provides the fuel that elevates the company. The success of the entire organization rests on SDRs' ability to create and qualify the right demand. There will be no deals to close or customers to serve without Sales Development. SDRs make a direct impact on a company's top-line number, valuation and it's success.

Regularly reinforcing the import and impact of the role helps Millennials to put their work within context of your broader business and gives them a mission with which to tie themselves.

Additionally, for the younger generation, sales usually needs to make an impact beyond making money for the business. Note to SDRs that Sales Development can also make a large impact outside of your company as well, with the customers and the people they serve.

Having customer case studies to share with Millennials brings to life the impact they could have on prospects. The younger generation wants to make a positive impact on society and the world, so tying them directly to some of your most interesting deployments can make that real.

For instance, an SDR once sourced a deal with NASA -- helping them understand their data and equipment in the mission to colonize Mars. This is no trivial feat; an SDR has helped to colonize a planet! Tying an SDR's work to this outcome can be rewarding for the individual contributor, the team and potential recruits.

It is the context and broader value of their work that drives Millennials. Find a way to tell and reinforce that story.

Side Note: Executive Translation

It can be hard for executives to bridge the generation gap. Coaching the executives before addressing a millennial workforce goes a long way to making the experience a positive one for all involved.

Take the tips provided in this chapter to help coach executives on addressing the team. Remind them to always provide context, link to impact, and give only actionable feedback.

Help executives be frank on the challenges the team is facing and remind them of the specific steps being taken to address the problems.

Young professionals expect that if an executive is speaking to them that they are briefed in on how the group is doing and what's going on.

Without proper preparation it is better to **not** have executives engage with young workers, as the disconnect can decrease credibility and lower morale.

Part 2: Motivate the Individual

Millennials understand the wealth of choices out there for them more than any generation before them. They are push notification away from the newest job details of their expanding universe of friends and connections.

Many of them haven't developed a clear picture of who they want to be or where they want to go with their careers. In fact, many of them are just learning what all the options might be!

Find how each individual SDR is motivated and help them explore interesting career paths. This starts early, during the interview, but should be an ongoing conversation. Coach young professionals to take time to understand themselves - they haven't done this yet.

Taking personality tests or strengths-finder is a good first step. Regularly asking insightful questions to understand and validate also helps:

- When was your best/worst day at work? Why?
- What do you most look forward to at work? Why?
- What are you passionate about? Why?
- What does success look like to you in 2 years? 5 years? 10 years?
- What is your personal mission statement?
- What impact do you want to make? Why?
- What's your MSA? Why?

Get to the bottom of why they do the things they do, and find a tie-in back to what they do today or what they can be building towards tomorrow.

Motivation relies on how SDRs frame **why** they are doing what they are doing.

Part 3: The Team Contract

Our team found it meaningful to develop a contract between management and the team to fully express our mission, values and commitment to each other.

This is *page one* in my team's playbook and forms the foundation to our daily interactions.

Here is a version of what I would write as a contract:

Our mission is to train, develop and become a world class SDR organization, which will set the new standard for the enterprise software industry. As a team, we have three goals for this year:

1. Creating and qualifying 4X qualified pipeline through deterministic demand.
2. Developing a bench of talent to feed our company.
3. Innovating on, executing and spreading demand-gen best practices.

The team's core values are built on a foundation of **integrity** and a commitment to always **do the right thing**. They are designed with an expectation of striving for **excellence** in every interaction, and commitment to constant improvement and growth as individuals and as a team.

We expect that success will occur through a commitment to **earning it** and doing what it takes to be successful. Finally, SDR leadership will hold the team **accountable** for personal and team performance, and we expect individual contributors to do the same of their leadership and peers. Our five core values are defined below:

- **Integrity**: a personal commitment to and congruence with our values.
- **Do the right thing**: for your team, yourself, your prospect, and your company.
- **Excellence**: continuously exceeding expectations with exceptional execution in every situation; Consistent performance and continuous advancement.
- **Earn it**: perseverance to achieving team and personal success.

- **Accountability**: doing what you say and holding others to the same standard.

SDR Managers and SDR ICs each have a contract to the team:

Manager - As a manager it is my duty to develop, empower and push my team forward. I will provide my team with an environment in which they can be successful and remove obstacles from their path while holding them accountable. I trust that my direct reports will do their best to exceed my expectations, and I will commit to their personal and professional growth so that they can achieve success.

SDR - As an SDR, it is my duty to exceed any goals or expectations set by my manager, challenge and innovate on the team's status quo, and strive to perform at my best in all I do. I trust that my manager will do his best to develop my skills and represent my interests.

Once each person understands the goal of the organization, their role and trusts each team member to be held accountable -- the path clears for execution with **excellence**.

Acting with integrity, transparency, and commitment to do the right thing will build trust, empowering managers and SDRs to hold each other mutually accountable. With this foundation, our team can move toward a common vision and perform at excellence.
--
Creating a contract for your team can provide a great deal of clarity; it is a vision to strive to and a mission to fulfill. It is important that this vision be your own, created with guidance and input from your team. Filling in ad-libs is meaningless.

With a strong set of core values and an understanding of each other's roles, it is much easier to have "tough" conversations - they, in essence, turn into guided self-reflections. Accountability and clarity are built into the very essence of the group. A culture with nowhere to hide creates a stage upon which to shine. This applies both to your leadership team and individual contributors.

Side Note: The Power of Defining Roles

One such instance particularly jumps out to me where defining roles had a powerful impact on one of my managers.

One of the groups she had been leading had been performing quite poorly. In fact, a lack of infrastructure and core values had led to a team that was visibly upset every day. You could tell in their body language and snide remarks that they were not bought in.

Often, this negative culture comes from one person who acts as the cancer - but in this case it was multiple team members! To top it off, a couple of the SDRs had decided to leave, but not before bad-mouthing leadership as they did so.

My manager was beside herself. She was a perfectionist, a hard worker that strove to help her team at every turn. How could they turn on her like that? She felt the visceral betrayal of her own former comrades rejecting her, literally leaving her team and poisoning it on their way out.

When she first approached me, I simply reminded her of her role; she was there to empower, champion and set her team up for success. They had an obligation to not only take from her, but to give back to her and the team as well. She should not bear the sole weight for their failure in attitude and performance. They were as responsible to her, the team and their own success as she was. This revelation so startled her that she began to cry - in realization and relief.

At first, she had spoken as if the weight of pulling the team firmly rested on her two shoulders. When we left the 1:1 she could see each member of the team, herself included, pulling their own weight and lifting each other together.

A newfound sense of empowerment followed and the team responded to a stronger, more confident leader who was willing to hold them accountable.

Part 4: Coach the Coaches

Many SDR managers have very little experience with management in general. In fact, since many are promoted from the SDR position, large portions of SDR managers are first-time managers.

Often, it is the star individual contributor who is chosen to become the manager. Unfortunately, the ability to over perform an individual quota does not necessarily make for the ability to effectively manage a team. Creating demand in a territory gives these first-time managers credibility, but not the skills to handle a team.

With new managers it is important to coach them on 4 main things: hiring, training, coaching and providing mutual accountability.

First-time can especially struggle with holding their teams accountable in a healthy manner.

As we've covered the hiring and training in detail in Part I and Part II, let's focus on coaching and accountability.

Coach the Coaches: Data-Driven Coaching
It helps to already be great at the core SDR skills to show individual contributors how to do the job, but it is even more important to know how to use data **so you know what to coach and why**. Good coaching provides actionable insights to improve performance using data-driven analysis and experience.

Coaches need to be able to understand their sales funnel, conversion metrics and gain insights through data to help SDRs correct course. First, this requires a rigorous system of measurement, monitoring and analysis.

From lead follow-up, email open, click-through, account penetration, opportunity reject, meeting to opportunity and opportunity to close rates -- an excellent coach not only teaches how, but measures why.

The rise of data in sales directly mirrors the rise of statistical analysis driving on-field strategy in major American sports, like baseball and basketball. More and more coaches are data analysts, turning raw data into coachable moments.

For instance, if a coach saw an abnormally high email reply rate he should think through several questions:

- What is the subject line and content of the emails the SDR is sending?
- What is the volume of email sent?
  - Are they logging all of their email activity?
  - Are they sending enough emails?
- Who are they sending emails to?
  - Are these "cold" contacts?
  - Are these only "warm" contacts via leads?
- Which Cadences are they sending these emails through?
  - Is the cadence to a specific company, use case or vertical?
  - Does the cadence target specific titles?
  - Is the email early on in the cadence or late? After how many touches?
- When are they sending the emails, at what time of day?

Although a high email reply rate can indicate a great content, it can also mean that an SDR is:

- Not sending enough emails
- Not logging all their emails - only the replies
- Only sending emails only to prospects who expect contact (warm leads)
- Sending extremely poor email content, logging unsubscribe replies

The myriad of metrics and conversion rates each require measurement. An understanding of the territory strategy and close examination to execution is necessary to produce precise and actionable insights.

For each of your core metrics, develop a system to record, monitor and interpret. As with the SDR Playbook, a Coach's Playbook can help to institutionalize this knowledge.

The important part is to begin to use data in addition to observation to drive your analysis.

Coach the Coaches: Mutual Accountability

One of the most important skills first-time managers lack is their ability to have "difficult" conversations - holding SDRs accountable.

As an individual contributor SDR, they were able to get ahead by pleasing all parties. When they blow out their quota everyone was happy - their team, AEs and managers.

The world changes quite a bit when they are moved into the management role - it is now their responsibility to hold their team accountable. Not only is the concept new to them, but they have yet to build the confidence to be able to do so.

First-time managers need to be coached to have honest conversations with their SDRs, especially in the first few months after their promotion. After all, not too long ago they were peers and friends with the same people they are managing today. Earning the respect to lead that very same team can be a struggle. So it is vital to be hands-on during this time, reviewing manager interactions, 1:1s and relationships.

One of the mistakes I've often made is not understanding what's happening in the relationships between the reps and the managers by purely relying on information from the managers themselves. Skip-level meetings are vital, especially as your new managers ramp into their role.

I can remember a specific instance when a star performer suddenly started to struggle. Personally, I chocked it up to a lack of motivation as the team grew and he had less of our collective attention. The bias was to trust my managers - they are, of course, those I work most closely with on a day-to-day basis and those I personally backed into leadership positions. There must have been something wrong with the rep's motivation, so I never took the time to truly listen to his concerns about the relationship with the manager. That was a mistake. Years later, I found this individual contributor having wild success working under different management - continuing the overperformance he initially had.

Many aspects go into performance, but do not overlook the significance of a SDR's working relationship with their manager. A relationship based on mutual accountability and trust is vital to the success of the team.

You and your managers should be building trust with regular 1:1s and coaching sessions (role play, recorded calls and email template reviews) while providing detailed, actionable feedback to your reps. This is the give in the give-to-get relationship.

Providing regular feedback takes investment and time from your managers. In doing so, they should be able to hold the SDRs to blowing out their quota.

Part 5: Agile Professional Development

There is no one topic more talked about or misunderstood than Professional Development in the Sales Development world. There are three fundamental misunderstandings: feedback cadence, structure and transparency.

Agile Professional Development: Feedback Cadence
Millennials are ready to grind. They are ready to work hard and to work smart. The difference with this generation is that they expect regular feedback. This stems from a deep desire to succeed and improve. Continuous improvement, they innately understand, only comes from receiving and acting on feedback.

Like Agile Development has sped up the release of code (think Facebook releasing code every day) - so too do millennials expect regular feedback at a much quicker pace. Using your critical thinking to provide this once a year in an annual review is no longer enough - this cadence is too slow in the information age.

Build a framework to give feedback on a bi-weekly or monthly cadence and hold your management team accountable to delivering on this. Not only does this fulfill expectations, but also a shorter cadence will increase the pace of growth of your team. This is the rise of Agile Professional Development. The millennial generation is ready to work harder and smarter than ever, but only if you're willing and able to do the work to challenge them to it.

In addition to feedback in a regular cadence, SDRs expect the feedback to be specific and actionable. This takes work and critical thinking for management. Here's a specific example that may be familiar to you:

An SDR, Steven, underperforms for the month, 50% of quota. It's been noticed that Steven has been playing a lot of ping-pong lately.

Traditional Manager: Steven, you had a really bad month. What happened? (Meaning: Give me an explanation)

Steven: I know, it was a rough month. I didn't get many leads. (Meaning: I know! I feel terrible about it, but I don't know why I failed.)

Traditional Manager: You should be able to hit quota without relying on lead flow - what happened to your pipeline? (Meaning: Excuses, excuses!)

Steven: It just wasn't there, you see I made the calls this month. I was #2 in activity! (Meaning: I tried hard though!)

Traditional Manager: Well, Steven, I've seen you playing a lot of ping-pong and not at your desk. Think about what you could have gotten done if you focused. I don't want to see you playing ping-pong anymore. (Meaning: I don't trust you to manage your time, you need to be baby-sat.)

Steven: OK. (Meaning: I've stopped listening, you aren't helping me get to my number this month.)

Now let's see what a manager who is providing specific and actionable feedback using active listening can accomplish:

SDR Manager: Steven, let's review last month. How'd you think it went?

Steven: Not well. I didn't get the usual number of leads and I wasn't able to hit quota -- which I really want to turn around this month.

SDR Manager: What, specifically, was your attainment against quota?

Steven: I went 5 for 10. At least 4 additional meetings fell through or pushed as well.

SDR Manager: That sounds rough - no one likes to miss. Lead flow is out of your control, but time management - one of the skills we're working on in your skilling plan - is in your control. Let's take a look at your calendar together - how are you scheduling your call times?

Steven: Here's my calendar. Usually I come in to work around 8, and start my calling around 9. Sometimes meetings get in the way though, as you know.

SDR Manager: Your territory is in the Central time zone. Usually prospects are at their desk from 8-9 AM and 4-6 PM local time. Do you think if we adjusted your call times and blocked it off, that you'd be more effective?

Steven: Yes, that would probably help! Do you think skipping meetings is OK though?

SDR Manager: Well, call time is sacred and if you book it off the week before, people will schedule around it.

Steven: That's true. How else would you recommend optimizing my schedule?

This is a conversation that happens quite frequently with SDRs - their ability to proactively manage their time and eliminate distractions needs to be learned. Simple frameworks, like the Urgent-Not Urgent quadrant can be powerful guides for a new professional (and for old ones as well).

	Urgent	Not Urgent
Important	Call times Lead Follow-up Opp Notes 1	Territory Plan Training Strategic Projects 2
Not Important	3 4 Say no! Or push to later.	

Help SDRs correctly identify the type of work before them (1, 2, 3 or 4?) and empower them to say "No" to anything in the 3rd or 4th quadrant.

A manager that works to help SDRs regularly prioritize their work and time while keeping them accountable to their own goals delivers the type of value that will enhance their belief in his leadership.

By tying these skills into their professional development and skilling plan, managers can show specific and actionable steps to improve over time. And that's all Millennials are really asking for. It's really not that tough.

Because providing this level of feedback requires thought and time, the span of control for SDR managers should not exceed 7 SDRs to 1 manager.

Side Note: Emails are not Effectiveness
One very common mistake new professionals make early on in their career is feeling the need to be responsive to every email at all times. They mistake a fast email response time with productivity.

In reality, this is a false indicator. Becoming a slave to their inbox makes SDRs *purely responsive* to the world around them. Their ability to prioritize their time slips away with the constant click of a mouse or tap of a phone. They are no longer proactive. Other people, not them, are driving the priorities in their work life.

Secondly, constant email checking leads to burnout. It does not allow the space necessary to approach situations from new angles. Long-term fatigue will set in with an already over-stimulated brain.

Instead, have SDR's schedule out time for checking email (or check email for quadrant 1 tasks, but do not respond otherwise) and block time out to do their other important tasks like calling, emailing or building cadences.

Agile Professional Development: Levels
In addition to giving more regular feedback, you should develop a structure of levels that can give tangible goals on performance and skills for the SDRs to attain while they are within the SDR organization. These are micro-promotions.

However, do not develop micro-promotions solely in response to SDRs demanding promotions.

A good micro-promotion program should be thoughtfully laid out with a framework that will help SDRs gain skills to master their current role and begin to bridge the gap to future roles.

Side Note: Outbound v. Inbound SDRs
Many teams structure "outbound" SDRs as more senior than "inbound" SDRs. In addition to this being a misnomer in the world of Account Based Sales Development, I do not believe that this structure provides value. There are different skills necessary to master optimizing demand in a territory vs. a limited set of accounts - but these are parallel skills.

SDRs from either the ADR or MDR role should be able to develop the skills necessary to move on to roles outside the SDR organization. Because both roles receive leads and penetrate accounts, the difference between the two roles should be narrowing in any case.

I've found success in developing a definition of progression reliant on more than just time in role.

Level 1 - Trainee (SDR): developing the skills to hit quota.
Level 2 - Owner (SDR): demonstrated ability to own territory, core skills, and consistently hit quota.
Level 3 - Master (Sr. SDR): mastery of role, ability to expand business, innovates, provides leadership and goes above/beyond consistently.

Within each of these three levels there should be well-defined expectations on the skills required to master them. By giving SDRs a standard to work to, they have a concrete bar upon which to measure themselves.

When professional development conversations come up, you can always reference the framework.

Let's take a look at a conversation between a SDR, Blake - who has been with the company for 2 years - and his manager.

Blake: I think I'm ready for a promotion. When can I become an AE?

SDR Manager: OK - sounds like you feel like you've mastered the SDR role. Is that true?

Blake: I've been doing this for 2 years now, yes.

SDR Manager: Let's pull up your quota performance, can you show me YTD attainment?

Blake: Yes - I've missed the past couple of months...but it's because of my AEs! They are really difficult to work with.

SDR Manager: Over the past six months you're at 80% and below average compared to the team. Do you feel that demonstrates a complete mastery of the role?

Blake: No, I guess not.

Manager: What do you think you can do to prove you've mastered the position?

Blake: Blow out quota for the next quarter.

Manager: OK - how do you plan on doing that? What's your strategy to attack your accounts next quarter?

Blake: Well, I haven't really worked that out, but I'll work to increase my dials and emails. That should help.

Manager: That plan doesn't reflect much knowledge of your territory, ownership of your accounts or a researched point of view. Let's work on a plan to demonstrate all of those. When you can consistently hit quota - 6 months rolling above 100% - and demonstrate an ability to own your business, then we can talk about that interview. In the meantime, I can help you develop your territory plan. Deal?

Blake: Sounds good, I'll come back with a plan outline.

Now, Blake could or could not work out, but he has an actionable plan moving forward and clear line of sight on what needs to be done to earn what he wants. He isn't being strung along and knows exactly where he stands.

Turning the professional development conversation into an actionable territory or skill plan motivates and provides structure to the SDR; they can measure their progress against the plan week-to-week. If they are unable to meet the plan, they are more likely self-select out.

Structure, clear definitions, honest feedback and actionable plans go a long way to turn conversations around professional development into a positive experience for everyone.

Once an SDR is ready - well on their way to mastering the Sr. SDR role - it is the job of the manager to find openings that fit the SDR's professional goals and to find/communicate a realistic timeline.

Just like qualifying a deal, SDR managers must qualify whether there's budget, authority, need and timeline for the desired role. Then, they should agree to evaluation criteria and an execution plan for the interview.

Once this is agreed upon with the hiring manager or HR, then the SDR manager can go back and coach their SDRs to the interview. It is critical to outline this process and engage the proper stakeholders early so that it is repeatable and scalable.

The interview should take place in parallel with the SDR completing her skilling plan and should be timed so the two fit as neatly as possible.

That being said, it is critical to set expectations with SDRs that *fit and business need are two separate things*. They may be a fit and have acquired the requisite skills, but business need - when positions are available - is an element that is outside of their control or their manager's.

Coaching new graduates and SDRs to professional patience - understanding and moving at the pace of the business - will help them in the long and short term with professional development. Good planning, transparency and clear communication make all the difference here.

Note that by demonstrating mastery of their role, the SDR *earns an interview*. However, in no way does the SDR earn the position until successfully interviewing. Make this abundantly clear.

With access to the hiring manager and internal champions, SDRs should never perform poorly at the interview.

Agile Professional Development: Transparency
In addition to full transparency on position openings, it is critical to be transparent on performance expectations and qualitative review. Many times, it can be intimidating for SDR managers to call out a specific timeline until promotion or performance expectation - however that is exactly what SDRs need to manage their expectations and measure themselves.

For instance, a central tenant in my evaluation is "consistent performance". It is important to detail what that means exactly. 6 months of continuous performance above quota? 2 years? Is it OK to have bad months, as long as it averages out? You need to be clear and transparent as to what your personal definition of success is.

Whatever it is, the most important thing is to have it defined and expressed to the team. This gives clarity. The worst scenario has no standard definition of performance. This will result in confusion for everyone. Promotions will be given to SDRs simply because they have tenure or, worse, there will be no promotions at all.

Have the courage to take a stand on the issue. Your definition of success is not a promise to promote, rather it is a clear expectation to fulfill. The promise is that once they fulfill your definition of success, that you will be their champion. And that's all they can really ask for.

CHAPTER 7
COMPENSATION

Next to professional development, SDR compensation confuses executives the most.

When not seeing the results they want from their SDRs, executives often change the comp structure. One organization I joined had changed comp 4 times in 9 months!

Obviously, at that point, the organization and the SDR team was not deriving value from the compensation plan. Mainly, they were confused. Our coin-operated team didn't have a clear understanding on how they were going to get paid. How tragic.

There are a few things to keep in mind when designing SDR compensation:
1. For many SDRs, this is their first job.
2. SDRs joined Sales to make money. They are coin operated.
3. Keep it simple, for everyone's sake.

When it comes to money, everyone wants to get it right. However, in execution it can often be unclear and delayed.

How often have you received a commission check, but don't know exactly why that's the bottom-line number? Or how often has commission been delivered late? Can you think of the last time your company has had to true-up?

These little wrinkles not only take time and resources to resolve, but erode the SDR team's confidence in leadership and the company. A clear, simple commission plan that ties directly to the results that you seek to accomplish is your best bet.

In addition to a clear plan, teaching SDRs how to read their commission statements and reconcile that with their earnings and bank statements will go a long way to reducing tension.

Remember, many of the SDRs are working their first jobs and need to be taught the basics about tax withholdings and rates. This can be especially difficult when managing a global team, so be sure you're up to date on the latest local laws when opening up coverage in Europe or Asia.

Lastly, it is imperative to offer competitive OTEs with other highly lucrative industries to attract the level of talent necessary to execute on Account-Based Sales Development. It is not uncommon to see experienced SDRs make six figures one or two years out of school.

This cost can be mitigated with a base/variable split that mirrors typical sales - 60% base & 40% variable. With proper management and audit, this will ensure that success and cost correlate.

Part 1: The Commission Plan
Part 2: It's a MONTHLY quota
Part 3: Other Rewards and Gamification
Part 4: Opportunity Audit = Quality Control

Part 1: The Commission Plan

To keep things simple, individual contributor compensation plans should have no more than 2 parts: Sales Accepted Leads (SALs or stage 2 opportunities) and Closed-Won sourced business. I am not a fan of paying for meetings, as they are often unqualified and do not result in real pipeline or revenue. If the goal of Sales Development is to produce qualified pipeline that turns into revenue, then a rigorous definition of an opportunity needs to be laid out. We'll explore this further with Bi-Modal Qualification in Part IV.

SAL Points

After mixing and matching for years, I believe that 100% OTE focused on SALs is most effective - as long as management audits opportunities for quality control and to ensure that there is minimal AE-SDR hand washing.

Furthermore, with SALs, a very basic point structure can have a drastic impact on focusing on your ideal target profile. It is important not to over-complicate this structure, however, as the reality of dirty data and complexity can have a big impact on the understanding and execution (and therefore effectiveness) of the plan.

Multi-variable point structures (using title, revenue, industry, etc.) can be confusing, gamed and depend on data that's often locked down or out of SDR control. Choose the most important variable to build a point structure around and maintain the cleanliness of that field.

A simple point system that has worked for companies looking to move up market can focus on revenue size or employee count. Revenue size was the most important shift for my teams as they began to move from the SMB to the Enterprise market. Here's a sample point plan:

Enterprise - Accounts above $1Bn in revenue = 2 points
SMB - Accounts below $1Bn = 1 points

By implementing a simple point system similar to the one above, my team's demand mix drastically changed. The number of opportunities in Enterprise accounts increased by over 100% in one month! It's not news, but it bears repeating; compensation is the #1 driver of behavior.

Additionally, a point structure like this unleashes the power of your Market Response team, by focusing them on creating demand where it means the most for your company. Secondarily, this shakes them out of their mindset of lead processing and empowers them to go after higher-value accounts.

If this is the type of behavior you are looking for, then do so by making it the sole focus of the compensation plan. It is singular and easily checked. Multivariable point systems suffer from a lack of confidence in all of the fields necessary to accurately assess an opportunity's grade. Additionally, compensation schemes can all be gamed, so design one that can be easily checked.

A complete focus on SAL creation also creates friction in the pipeline, good friction. SDRs are always creating more opportunities -- and that's a good thing for the company!

When some AEs are more concerned with sandbagging - er, pipeline management - than with fielding all the demand - a forcing function to create pipeline will ensure healthy long-term coverage.

Sales management needs to force these opportunities to be created in order to fully understand where and how demand is currently being produced. They can adjust coverage accordingly, but cannot do so without the visibility of the demand being created in the first place.

Closed-Won Bonus
The second portion of compensation should include a portion that is tied to the quality and outcome of SDR work. Typically, the end result we are looking for is closed-won business.

Tying compensation to outcome not only incentivizes SDRs to do good work in the right accounts, but also fosters a sense of teaming with their AEs. When their partners win, the SDR will win and that's psychologically important.

However, SDRs can often feel far removed from the ability to close business -- and in enterprise deals they certainly are! After they pass an opportunity it can take a year until a deal closes.

For this reason, I believe the closed-won portion of compensation should rest in a bonus structure above the SAL variable. For me this is best compensated with a bonus close to 1% of a deal with a $100k deal minimum (to drive ASP).

Here's an example:
$0-$100K: $0 Bonus
$100K-$250K: $1,000 Bonus
$250K-$500K: $2,500 Bonus
$500K+: $5,000 Bonus

You may need to adjust accordingly to your business and average selling price.

Part 2: It's a MONTHLY quota

Sales Development should be managed in monthly sprints to best produce an even, predictable increase in pipeline.

As previously mentioned, total group cost (including tooling and management compensation) should one tenth of forecasted closed pipeline sourced. In order to support the 10x SDR multiple, each SDR should achieve a 12-15x multiple against their compensation cost every year.

So, if Unicorn Dash is paying their SDRs $100K OTE, the average SDR should be expected to source $1.2M of business per year to be economically viable. This directly impacts quota:

Monthly Quota = 12x OTE * (1/ASP) * (1/12 months) * (1/Close Rate)

Let's say we're still working with Unicorn Dash - who has a $100K average selling price and a 10% close rate from stage 1 opportunity.

Monthly Quota = $1.2M / $100K ASP * (1/12 months) * (1/.10)
Monthly Quota = 10 SALs

Now it's important to note that you need your SDRs to produce 10 *raw* SALs every month.

In the compensation model developed earlier, you are rewarding SDRs on SAL *points*. This may not directly correlate to the number of raw SALs they produce if the mix isn't exactly what you anticipate.

You should forecast raw SALs to the business, while using points as a method to get there. Keeping track between the raw and point difference will help you understand if you need to tweak your point structure or assumptions moving forward.

In the enterprise space an average ADR typically produces 8-10 raw SALs while MDRs can produce 12-15.

Part 3: Other Rewards and Gamification

Leveraging competitions, SPIFFs, Awards and Gamification can be extremely motivating for SDRs. These can provide transparency, a sense of teaming and clear purpose.

In the grind of the work year, these can also provide concrete "beginnings" and "endings" around which your teams can sprint.

As with compensation plans, it is vital to keep these simple and do them one at a time. SPIFFs have diminishing marginal returns and if there are too many running at the same time, SDRs will not understand which one to focus on.

Competitions & SPIFFs

SDRs are naturally competitive and it's important to harness this in a positive fashion.

Competitions set-up by management should focus on the team, either between teams or the team against a discreet goal. The focus on teaming will force ICs to hold each other mutually accountable. It also allows more of the group to "win" vs. individual competitions in which usually only 2-3 (of the same) SDRs will be in the running to win. When teams naturally begin to compete against each other, you know you're on the right track and have good leadership in the trenches.

Write them up on the board, send them in an email and constantly remind the SDRs. It's important to reinforce competitions to maximize the impact.

Secondly, publically acknowledge and celebrate SPIFF winners. Although SDRs may not admit it, recognition plays an important role in motivation for them.

Once you've set-up a simple structure, deliver on it consistently. This builds trust and confidence with the team.

Lastly, challenge your team leaders to build a culture of competition and creativity. Give them a small budget and have them build their own competitions or challenges. There's nothing more exciting than the buzz of their peers to further reinforce the importance and value of winning.

Anticipation of winning can be as rewarding as winning itself.

SDR Awards

Yearly and quarterly awards can also be motivating and generally showcase the values that your organization espouses. SDRs can often be overlooked at Sales Kick Offs (SKOs) as junior members of the sales organization, but it is vital to team morale to treat them as equals with their own set of awards.

Some awards that have worked in the past include:

SDR of the Year - SDR who most embodies SDR core values and a commitment to excellence

Coach of the Year - SDR who has most helped the others around them

Challenger Champion - SDR who most embodies the values of the *The Challenger Sale*

President of SDR President's Club - SDR who is #1 in quota attainment

Make sure to communicate these well before you give them - they are a statement of your values, a reward to your SDRs and a continuous aspirational goal for every member of your team.

Side Notes: Caution with Award and SPIFFs

Awards and SPIFFs lose effectiveness when not consistently executed upon. If you forget to give the award or hand-out the reward for winning, the team won't be sure about execution the next time around.

Make sure that you and your management team are committed and accountable to consistently delivering on the structure of your Award and SPIFF programs.

Event SPIFFs for SDRs

Often, SDRs are called to drive attendance to events. If not managed correctly, these can distracting and have poor ROI.

For instance, driving people to visit your booth at a large and diverse show like Dreamforce can be an arduous task that results in very few actual opportunities. However, a more targeted company-sponsored field event around Dreamforce can be a great source of pipeline.

For these latter events, a SPIFF that rewards SDRs for driving attendance will help to focus their activities. Typically a 4:1 compensation ratio of attendee to SAL point will ensure enough attention to the event.

Compensate only on those attendees who actually come to the event to ensure that SDR are driving quality results. MDRs typically have the most purview to drive attendance as they own the largest base of leads, while ADRs should leverage field events as a part of their account strategy and plan of attack each quarter.

SDRs need at least 6 weeks of notice to successfully recruit for an event in their territory. Depending on the target profile, you can typically expect around 30 registrants per MDR, 15-20 per ADR and a 75% attendance rate across the board. In larger cities where there are more competing events, like SF and NYC, attendance rate can lower into the 60% range. Using this data, you can accurately forecast the cost of a SPIFF program.

Gamification is Performance Management

For years, I didn't believe in gamification. And I still don't.

Gamification for the sake of gamification alone is meaningless. Badges, shiny screens and fancy music only make sense in the context of creating competition around *the right metrics*. Just creating a system of automated rewards isn't enough; it is a commitment to creating a competitive environment that will push SDRs to be more effective and which makes their day more enjoyable.

When gamification is paired with real data-driven metrics and a coaching staff trained to use it, then it is valuable. You can only keep SDRs interested in badges for so long.

An upfront investment to ensure that gamification tools integrate, measure and foot to the schedule of core metrics, SPIFFs and competitions is vital. This is another reason why it's so important to keep a consistent and straightforward framework -- aligning the supporting infrastructure takes time and resources.

We're just getting to the point of being able to measure volume metrics with effectiveness metrics in real-time. Until we're able to do so, gamification will continue to sit on the outskirts.

Part 4: Opportunity Audit = Quality Control

The last portion of compensation should be an audit program. SDRs in my teams are only compensated once an AE has accepted **and** a manager has approved their SAL. An audit of every opportunity passed accomplishes two things:

1. It ensures accountability by forcing SDR managers to check the quality of SALs passed.
2. It reveals coaching opportunities to help SDRs improve.

Audit will also inspire confidence within the SDR leadership team - when everyone knows that the SALs passed are 100% of quality, then it is much easier to hold Sales and MRKT accountable to their SLAs and goals.

The process to audit, and therefore pay on a SAL, should be as light as possible and seek to simply determine that the opportunity has met the qualification criteria. Once SDRs know that all of their work will be inspected for pay, the quality of their notes and activities logged will drastically improve.

Be careful to train managers on the use of audit, lest it become a tick-the-box activity. Opportunity notes are some of the best raw data to drive coachable moments because they reveal how an SDR qualifies, targets, internalizes information from their prospects and communicates with their AEs.

To keep SDR leaders honest, make sure to only pay them on audited opportunities as well. It is hard work for SDR management, reviewing hundreds of opportunities, but it is important and necessary work to ensure a high standard. Quality-control matters.

> **Side Note: Audit your own team. And only them.**
> Because it is mainly a tool for coaching, managers should be responsible for auditing **all** of their team's opportunities and **only** their own team's opportunities.

What coaching value are they getting when reviewing SALs from another team? Unless done as a leadership team exercise, regular cross-team auditing only corrodes trust among SDR leadership and should be avoided.

CHAPTER 8
ABSD Technology Architecture

Attention CMOs, COOs and Sales VPs: If you're looking to make the largest gains in the least amount of time, look no further than your core infrastructure - Salesforce. The most important relationship for any SDR leader is with their Marketing Operations team, as they sit right on top of this engine.

The process of lead routing, workflow, opportunity creation, field mapping and hand-off are the core of the revenue machine. They are also the processes which most leak. Like a broken septic tank in a creaking house, improper infrastructure design can make the whole place stink.

In order to maximize lead conversion rates and scale effectively, look to build an account-based, automated, monitored and airtight lead system.

Implementing Salesforce is not easy. Whenever I dig into a new environment, the number of black holes in the system is dramatic. Tens, even hundreds, of thousands of leads can sit unmanaged in queues or in the cold hands of long dead users.

In one specific example, opportunity hand-off was designed to be a two-step process. In the first step, an SDR would nominate a lead to become an opportunity. In the second, the AE was supposed to convert the lead into a contact and create that opportunity.

However, everyone was counting opportunity creation only after the first step. There was no oversight as to whether or not those leads were actually converted at all! This resulted in 10% of all opportunities leaking out of the pipe.

We lost 10% of all our future revenue on one broken process alone!

The result was millions of dollars thrown away because of one poor decision on design.

If you don't have your Marketo and Salesforce systems buttoned up, it will lead to gross inefficiencies and should be fixed as a first priority.

Since everything is automated or done in huge batches, without proper design you can quickly lose thousands of leads and hundreds of opportunities, leading to conversion rates in free-fall. Without a properly laid foundation from which to work, SDRs cannot do their jobs and the business will suffer for it. Your backyard will be a sewer before you know it.

For that reason, no lead should be left behind.

Part 1: Lead Creation and Routing
Part 2: Lead Workflow, Nurture & Management
Part 3: Lead to Opportunity Hand-Off

Part 1: Lead Creation and Routing

Lead routing should be designed with the following principle in mind:

Get the right leads to the right people in the least amount of time.

Let's break that down. Getting the right leads mean that your demand-gen team understands your ideal target profile and accounts to produce leads from the appropriate demand profile. These leads are ideas for which your SDRs should be using to determine if they should begin the process of account penetration.

When attacking the enterprise market, asking for leads to double every year you want to double revenue will not work. The value, quality and targeting of leads must increase over time and take priority over sheer quantity.

This may be concerning to Marketing or Executive management to see lead growth flatten over time, but it is the natural course of good Account-Based Marketing, which is not covered in this book.

The enterprise market is only so large, and so after a certain amount of time it is important to focus on quality and depth of leads.

Getting those leads to the right person means that the leads are routed to the person who would have the most knowledge about that account.

If an account is covered by an ADR, then leads from that company should directly routed to that ADR. If not, then a MDR should field the lead. Lead flow in a territory should be designed to follow the hybrid model:

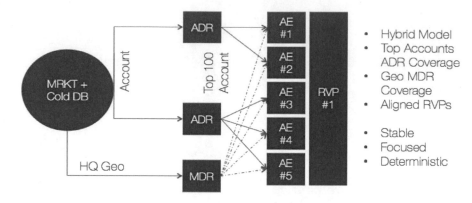

Lastly, leads should be routed in as little time as possible. The value of a lead decreases the older it is because prospects will move on to another competitors, topic or task.

Side Note: F*#! Fairness

Fairness should **not** play a key role in the design of lead routing.

Typically a market response SDR can field 300-400 leads per month max; if there are more leads in a territory then add more MDRs to it.

Focus on creating sales alignment over "fairness". MDRs should be directly aligned to a regional sales team's territory and should be able to supplement their lead flow by creating demand themselves. Because MDRs should be able to both process inbound leads and go outbound to create deterministic demand, they should be able to hit quota regardless of the number of leads which pass their way. Get them used to this mindset.

MDRs should be leveraging their knowledge of territory, industry expertise, AEs, events, partners and all other tools in their belt to accomplish their goal of crushing quota. Leads are simply one input to that larger plan to maximize demand in the territory.

In sales, territories will never be fair - covering even one section of California vs. all of Wyoming are two very different jobs. SDRs need to get used to that now.

Part 2: Lead Workflow, Nurture & Management

Designing an automated system which ensures all leads are properly routed, owned, nurtured and monitored is hard.

Usually, the devil is in the details as even one improperly managed step can result in thousands of leads lost or mismanaged.

Here's a simplified lead workflow architecture:

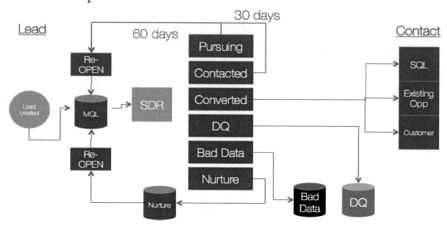

The purpose here is to ensure all MQL'd leads are sent to the appropriate SDR who will appropriately work or disposition the lead. SDRs should only own leads which they are actively working, or send the leads they are not working to a Nurture, Bad Data or Disqualifed queue for Marketing to manage.

One nifty trick to ensure that SDRs do not hoard leads is to automatically re-open any leads in their working buckets after a certain number of days. Since cadences are typic ally not designed for over 30 days, re-opening ensures that SDRs keep a clean pipeline by forcing them to re-evaluate stagnant leads.

At the core of lead management lay Lead Status and Queues. The following are the core lead status types I used:

- Type: Open
  - OPEN
  - Re-OPEN
- Type: Accepted
  - Pursuing
  - Contacted
  - Converted
- Type: Rejected
  - Disqualified
  - Nurture

Leads and contacts should always be assigned a lead or contact "Status" so that they can be segmented and reported on. These are critical indicators of SDR workflow and help us to understand how the lead and contact base is triaged. Make sure that your leads and contacts have similar statuses. Below the details of each status follow.

Lead Type: Open

Open leads have not been triaged (accepted or rejected), by any SDR. Set the expectation that all leads should be triaged by the end of each day.

Lead status	Definition
MQL	Raw item and no action has been taken; default status when leads come in or has had enough activity to re-qualify.
Open	A lead that has previously been set to an Accepted status, but has stayed there for over 60 days will automatically open. This forces SDRs to re-engage or clean out leads which have stagnated.

Lead Type: **Accepted**

Accepted leads are deemed to be of high enough quality for the SDR to work.

Lead status	Definition	Action
Pursuing	Contact attempted by the SDR, but not yet made.	Pursuing leads should be cleaned out at the end of every week, keeping only those which should be actively pursued.
Contacted	Had a conversation with the lead, but need further information to determine if it's qualified or not.	SDRs should set follow-up tasks to remember when to next contact these prospects.
Converted	If the lead was converted to a contact in an existing account or opportunity, then the lead is considered good enough to work and Sales-Accepted.	SDRs should convert these - either into accounts or new opportunities, as appropriate.

Lead type: Rejected

Rejected leads are leads that are deemed by the SDR to not be ready for engagement by the team at that time.

Lead status	Definition	Action
Bad Data	This is a lead which cannot be actioned at all. Unable to triangulate information, email or call.	These leads should not re-open or receive communications from Marketing. These should be routed to a Bad Data queue for review to be deleted. Routing: Bad Data Queue
Nurture	Lead which is not ready for engagement but should be nurtured by Marketing as appropriate.	The "Nurture" bucket serves as the company's pool to keep leads warm and continue marketing. These leads will be re-marketed to based on their individual characteristics. Once there is activity by the prospect, then the lead should re-MQL and be routed appropriately. Routing: Marketing Queue
Disqualified	This is a lead which comes from a competitor, Employee/Interviewee, or is otherwise outside our target profile.	These leads will not re-open or receive communications from Marketing. Routing: Disqualified Queue

Queues

Queues in Salesforce should be carefully managed to ensure that no leads are lost. Using a limited set will help to control lead management.

Routing (MQL) - this queue should be the main queue from which leads are temporarily sent to be routed to the appropriate SDR.
Marketing (Nurture) - this queue should hold the majority of leads - all leads which are within the ITP and should be marketed against.
Disqualified - this queue holds leads created from employees, interviewees, competitors and those outside the ITP. These leads may be useful later, for instance by partners.
Bad Data - this queue holds all spam leads and those without enough data to enrich. This queue should be manually reviewed and cleared for deletion.

The idea is to have SDR own all open leads in their territory and leads that they are currently working, *but no more*. Otherwise leads should rest with a MRKT queue to be appropriately marketed to.

To ensure that leads do not simply lag in an SDRs pipeline, set automatic re-open rules for working statuses. These rules will re-open leads after a set number of days and forces SDRs to keep a clean lead pipeline and make a decision on what should happen with their leads, ensuring they are properly managed.

An additional method to gain leverage in markets outside of the ITP would be to distribute those leads to a partner.

These partners may have domain expertise or simply have more time to pursue leads in smaller markets. Make sure to agree to a follow-up SLA and to set up follow-up monitoring to ensure these leads don't get lost.

Part 3: Lead to Opportunity Hand-Off

Once the lead architecture has been developed then it is time to look at the overall process for turning those leads into qualified opportunities. The design should ensure that there is ownership at every stage and that all pertinent information collected continues to be passed.

The quality of an SDR's notes are the work product which they produce and directly impact sales' close rates.

A simplified opportunity process is as follows:

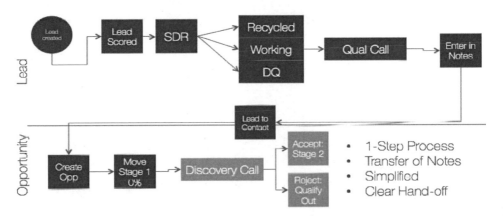

Of course, the work for a SDR shouldn't stop with what needs to be done in the CRM to get the information to the AE. She also needs to set-up a smooth transition for the prospect in hand-off.

SDRs should:

1. Send Introductory Email to the prospect introducing them to the Account Executive and setting out the initial agenda for the meeting.

2. Send Meeting Request to book Discovery Call with Prospect and Account Executive.

3. Schedule a preparation call with the AE.

4. Convert the lead into a contact and stage 1 opportunity.
Record *all* of the information gathered from the call and convert the lead to an opportunity. Additionally, provide a summary/analysis of what has been learned to be easily digested by AEs and internal executives.

The qualification form in the CRM should be so designed as to encompass all the qualification expectations that define an opportunity.

SDRs should understand that their ability to provide insightful notes form the core foundation to the value they are adding to their Account Executives and the company -- setting up a meeting is only part of an opportunity.

CHAPTER 9
EXECUTING ABSD IN PRACTICE

Architecting the back-end systems for Account-Based Sales Development forms the foundation of the system, but it is by no means the end. The swing that your SDRs use every day needs to mirror requirements of ABSD.

As opposed to simply processing leads, ABSD challenges SDRs to understand a prospect's company, the business outcomes desired and then to prescribe a solution with credible customer examples.

This section will cover the ability to research, find prospects and deliver customized messaging at scale - the process that is account penetration. Next, it will tackle the skills to write effective emails and have conversations with prospects to give and get value. Lastly, it evolves qualification criteria to allow SDRs to create demand in our ideal profile using *The Challenger Sale* principles.

Part 1: Account Penetration Process
Part 2: Cadence Types & Strategy
Part 3: Social Media
Part 4: Writing and Delivering Effective Emails at Scale
Part 5: Warm Calling
Part 6: Bi-Modal Qualification

Part 1: Account Penetration Process

Account Penetration is not a destination, it is a journey.

The land and expand model can leave a lot of value on the table if an account is considered to be penetrated on the first land. Often, the use case for an initial land is small and nothing more than a slightly larger paid proof of concept (POC).

Yet, too often an account is left to a single Customer Success Manager (CSM) once the initial deal has been closed.

Account Penetration is a process which the entire account team (AE, SDR, CSM) should coordinate to maximize the value of an account.

Target Accounts — Research — Build PPOV — Execute Cadence

Find Ideal Profile.   Provide value above expectations.   At scale.

In deciding on target accounts, segmentation by industry, revenue or use-case and the concurrent messaging will align the account penetration team on the strategy and tactics.

For some regions this can get very specific. For instance, if you know a certain competitor has many customers in New York, but is vulnerable due to a lack of product innovation - that will drive a key piece of Account Team's strategy in that specific territory.

Once the target profile is aligned, then it is up to the SDR to research the accounts and contacts to be targeted. In the case of our competitor strategy, SDRs should then use the tools available to determine the technologies used in accounts within their territory and select on those accounts with that technology.

Databases like DiscoverOrg and RainKing not only have contact information, but information on technologies as well. Job openings, expertise in LinkedIn or press releases may also contain intel on an account's technology landscape. SDRs should also analyze the lead base in their territory to understand which accounts might already be warm and fit within their strategy.

Target accounts should have an identified transformation, an urgent need for change at some level which your product can address.

> Remember: Enterprise SDRs should only identify up to 100 accounts to penetrate per quarter. Limiting the number of accounts ensures that SDRs stay focused on penetration and also limits the ability to simply claim a massive number of accounts to farm for leads.

Once accounts have been identified, the next step is to prospect the correct contacts within the account itself. Besides finding contact information to reach your prospects, the goal of doing research is to find a specific transformation or a trait in the account that fits the penetration strategy the SDR is pursuing.

PPOV build works on three levels: contact, account and industry.

- **Contact** - transformation or goals on a personal level. For instance, a CIO might state on her LinkedIn that she's an expert in "data-driven decision making" or a customer CTO may have recently changed his position to work for a competitor.
- **Account** - company-level strategies or challenges, often explicitly stated in 10-Ks, letter to investors or news articles on the company. These PPOVs often focus on how to deliver a competitive advantage (or mitigate a competitor's advantage) by executing on the company's strategy.
- **Industry** - general research on industry trends can provide a PPOVs as well. For instance, you can tie many platforms to help with the need for CPG companies to establish new markets in emerging economies.

This research forms the foundation to build our cadences. By combining what the SDR learned during research with what they know about the company's product and customer case studies, SDRs should be able to deliver a valuable, insightful and credible message to their prospect.

Part 2: Cadence Types & Strategy

Remember that buyers now want to complete 70% of their buying process *before* they engage with a vendor. Additionally, every person is now being bombarded with a higher volume of targeted messaging via different media sources every day. Twitter, LinkedIn, Snapchat, Instagram, Facebook, and Google (to name a few) compete with phone calls, texts, emails and voicemails for our attention every second we're not asleep or in the shower (and maybe even sometimes then).

That means that SDRs need to be continuously providing value in building and delivering PPOVs consistently over a longer period of time to earn the right of first engagement. In essence, SDRs need to execute targeted micro-marketing campaigns using a variety of touches to engage a contact. This is what is called a cadence.

To ensure they SDRs reach their prospects they should build and deliver several different types of cadences.

The 4 Types of Cadences	Broad PPOV	Specific PPOV
Broad Audience	Catch All Cadence	Industry Cadence
Specific Audience	Use-Case Cadence	Account Specific Cadence

Teams which prospect for highly-complex enterprise platforms often face the daunting task of finding the most applicable message across a variety of potential benefits, use-cases and industries. The four main types of cadences delivered to enterprise accounts depend on the content and audience targeted.

Use-Case Cadences - focus on how a specific function or title could get value from our product. For instance, Sales Operations teams across all types of accounts could use Sales Analytics.

Industry Cadences - tie in the prevailing trends within in an industry to how the product can impact them. For instance, the news and media industry face increasing competition from digital channels, they need to better segment and market using their customer data to survive.

Account Specific Cadences - are tailored and unique to a specific account. They use research that would apply only to that account and the contacts being prospected. For example, SDRs should know that a newly-appointed CEO of a Pharmaceutical Company has publically stated that she plans growth through M&A and use that to engage her entire organization.

"Catch All" Cadences - use the company's main messaging and target a broad audience where a Use-Case or Industry campaign does not apply, and for low value accounts which do not merit their own cadence to be built. This is the cadence of last resort.

Marketing and SDR leadership should help with building Catch All, Industry and Use-Case specific cadences. The content from these types of cadences can be copied and easily executed by the entire team. Although they are good, they paint in broader strokes.

For top accounts, individual contributor SDRs should use their deep research to develop as many Account Specific cadences as they can successfully execute. Enterprise SDRs should be using most of their time building Account Specific cadences as this provides the most unique insights and value to their prospects. It's like building an individualized teaching plan, tailored content is always more effective. Building and delivering Account Specific cadences at scale forms the core of executing ABSD to individual SDRs.

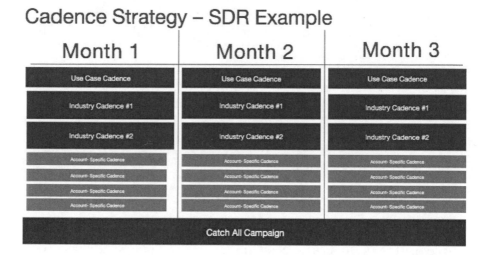

SDRs should have a strategy on the number and type of cadences they plan to execute every month. In the above cadence schedule, the orange cadences were built for the SDRs and they were encouraged to build as many grey cadences as they could deliver while meeting their activity goals. The focus is to produce *quality activity at scale*.

Each cadence will convert at different rates, so it is important to run a variety of cadence types to diversify risk. Highly complex software solutions have a variety of applicable use-cases, so having a variety of cadence types allows an SDR to engage their market from every available angle.

Beyond the content strategy, SDRs should understand the goal of each of their cadences to determine its design. Are they looking for a bottom-up referral, top-down referral or go direct to a mobilizer?

	Bottom-Up	Top-Down	Direct
# of Contacts	High	Low	Low
# of Touches	Medium (Email)	High (Email + Social)	High (Phone + Email + Social)
# of Strong PPOVs	Low	High	High
Goal	Referral	Referral	Opportunity
Cadence Type	•Catch-All •Use-Case	•Industry •Account-Specific	•Account-Specific

Bottom-up cadences can be shallower, targeting a wide range of contacts within an account with the goal of getting referred to the right person. This tactic works well when not much is known about an account, the decision maker is unclear or the account is not squarely in the ITP and does not merit a large investment. Use-case specific cadences also work well, as they speak to how to deliver value to a specific function.

For instance, an SDR prospecting to sell a training tool might reach out to the sales team about how they can help crush quota, with the goal of reaching the sales enablement mobilizer.

Top-down cadences typically try to get a response from an executive to a trusted person on his staff to investigate an SDR's PPOV. These executives are difficult to reach but typically understand the company's broader business strategy. They are the best to align vision with, but do not have the time to tactically evaluate or execute. Typically, industry cadences are attractive because they attach a potential solution to well-known overarching trends that executives are aware of.

The same SDR selling a training tool might point to the trend in the industry of adoption *The Challenger Sale*, something executives might have passing knowledge of. That would, hopefully, broker an introduction with the sales enablement team.

Direct targeting to known mobilizers require a measure twice and cut once mentality. Since these are the people you want to reach, it is worth the time to invest in account-specific cadences.

Whether direct targeting or going top down, putting in more work to develop account-level PPOVs is worth the effort to produce well qualified opportunities.

By using the three types of cadences, an SDR can effectively surround a single account by attacking from multiple angles.

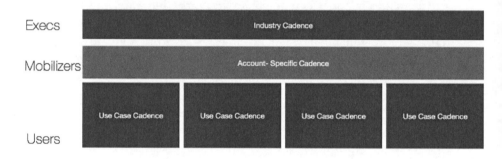

Using Multiple Cadence to Attack an Account

Using this concept, MDRs should mainly find the correct Use-Case cadence to put their leads into, since they are probably not mobilizers. Then, they should work to prospect further into qualified accounts to deliver account-specific or industry level cadences to mobilizers and executives.

This is how lead as an idea is executed.

Side Note: The New Intersection of MRKT & SD
As the industry moves to ABSD and the delivery of account specific content through SDR cadences, there arises a closer need for MRKT engagement to develop messaging.

The new mesh point will be in building cadences with account-specific content and messaging. SDRs have become the scalpel upon which MRKT can slice into an account. They are the most effective, powerful and persistent medium a MRKT department has to go to market.

Great product marketing teams and other subject matter experts can provide the credibility needed to turn a mediocre cadence into a highly relevant and thought-provoking line of reasoning. They can quickly insert in the jargon, insights and context that matter.

SDRs should working side-by-side with product marketing and company thought-leaders to develop their cadences. I'm a big advocate of assigning PM-SDR pairs to create and test cadences. Once they're proven to be successful, they can quickly be shared and executed on by the rest of the team.

Part 3: Social Media

One of the things that benefited MuleSoft was our quick adoption of Social Media. In 2014, MuleSoft was one of the top 3 Bay Area prospecting teams on LinkedIn. Social media has become central to prospecting, it is in our DNA.

A connection request itself can be a refreshing, different and personal channel with which to bring a PPOV to mind. By being intentional on the message to connect and subsequent InMails, SDRs can provide value from different angles.

Additionally, LinkedIn profiles should be optimized to showcase an SDR's ability to help prospects with their business. Powerful recommendations from form prospects, a professional picture and a profile which centers on providing value to customers (vs. sales accomplishments) can make a LinkedIn profile be a second landing page.

Hosting content on the profile shows thought leadership and builds an SDRs credibility. With more access to a salesperson's information than ever before, prospects should be assured with an intelligent, customer-oriented LinkedIn profile.

Twitter can also be another resource and alternative method of research/contact. Usually corporate executives can be found there, and using this to follow and build on their ego can be an effective method of driving engagement.

In the end, cadences should be built with the goal of having prospects understand the PPOV being delivered. By giving this value, SDRs will earn the right to a qualification call.

Tools like SalesLoft and Outreach.io help SDRs to build, organize and deliver cadences at scale. Mastering the skills to use tools like these, now form the core of an SDR's job.

Part 4: Writing and Delivering Effective Emails at Scale

In this section we will explore the basic concepts of writing effective emails, which is the main method with which SDRs communicate their PPOVs within their cadences.

I use the following rubric to evaluate the effectiveness of an email:

Content Accuracy: Does the email deliver content true to your company's messaging, positioning and product?

Well-researched: Does the email demonstrate an ability to find and effectively message around relevant information about the prospect?

Concise: "I didn't have time to write a short letter, so I wrote a long one instead."- Mark Twain.

Articulate: "Don't use a five-dollar word when a fifty-cent word will do." - Mark Twain

Correct Grammar: Does the email use correct English?

Engagement: Does the email effectively engage the prospect with compelling messaging and content?

Call to Action: Is there a clear call to action in the email?

There are three different type of emails which SDRs should produce:
1. PPOV Emails
2. Follow-up Emails
3. Break-up Emails

The core of providing value lies in the ability to quickly build effective PPOV emails to deliver in a cadence.

Email Type: PPOV Emails
A great PPOV email can include up to 7 core value points that flow in the following logic.

7 Email Value Points

1. A compelling **reason** to reach out
2. The relationship between that **reason** to a **value prop**
3. Relevant product **functionality** to deliver the **value prop**
4. **Customer story** demonstrating that **functionality**
5. **Result** from **customer story**
6. Prospect's **potential gain** if given a **result**
7. Why you, Why you now?

Professional prospecting emails build credibility and deliver a PPOV in an articulate and concise manner.

My teams use three types of PPOV emails in order to change tone, intensity and level of investment in a contact. A high PPOV email will use as many value points as possible.

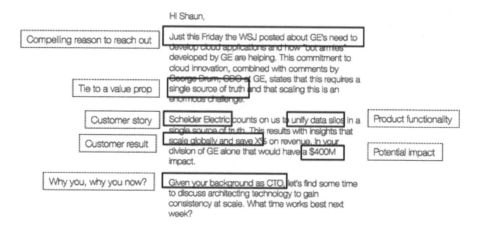

A medium or low PPOV email will use less value points. These are easier to produce in higher volumes and can be easier to digest by prospects.

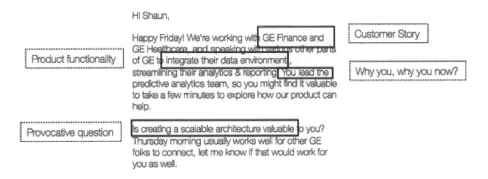

Bringing different levels of PPOV intensity throughout the cadences ensures that SDRs sound like humans, and not a marketing engine. Each of the three cadence strategies (top-down, direct and bottom-up) has different levels of intensity.

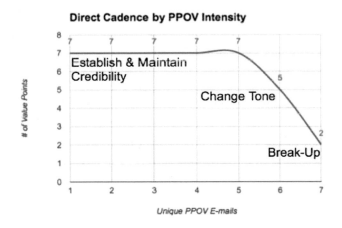

Cadences going Direct to mobilizers take the most time and research to complete. Because these prospects are the most knowledgeable about your space, it is more difficult to earn credibility and deliver new insights. For this reason, a high intensity cadence is necessary to elicit engagement.

So, Stephanie, the SDR, who is selling a CRM, would find the COO, Head of Operations and Director of Sales Operations and put them into a Direct cadence to receive a sustained high-intensity set of emails (and calls).

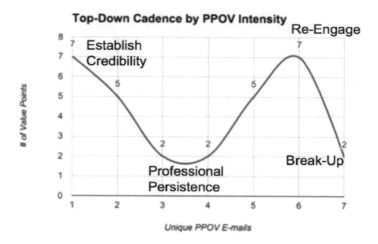

Unique PPOV E-mails

With a Top-Down strategy, SDRs need to earn credibility quickly and show professional persistence with busy executives. These executives have great business knowledge and context, but less domain expertise so the depth of value does not need to be maintained. Since the goal is to earn a referral, it is often enough to deliver several lower intensity emails simply to remind executives to execute a referral.

In this situation, Stephanie targets the CEO, CRO and all the VPs of Sales with a Top-Down cadence, varying the intensity with a persistent cadence to get to her goal of getting a referral to the Head of Operations or other mobilizer.

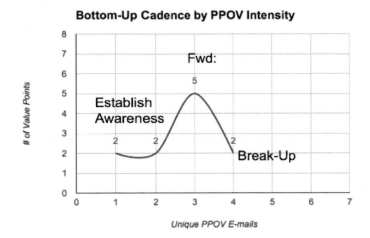

Bottom-Up Cadence by PPOV Intensity

A Bottom-Up strategy focuses on a high volume play across the organization. Establish awareness with low intensity emails to many contacts in order to get the organization talking about your product. The middle of the cadence provides enough value in an email for it to be forwarded to the correct person. Since the majority of the prospects in this cadence are not qualified, it isn't necessary for it to be as deep or intense. Volume is the name of the game here.

Stephanie targets all of the salespeople and sales operations analysts with this Bottom-Up cadence to establish a ground swell of support/awareness and to get a referral up to the correct person. She can also validate her PPOV more thoroughly at the lower levels, finding and exposing pain the executives or mobilizer might not even be aware of.

PPOV Email: Subject Lines

Subject lines are one of the most important parts of the email; they drive open rates. Subjects should be short and tailored to the prospect or the account. Using "re:" on reply emails also increases open rates.

Used carefully, spelling or capitalization mistakes can also increase open rates by indicating that the email has been written by a person direct to the prospect, and therefore is not a mass-marketing email. Non-html emails tend to work better for the same reason.

A few examples of good subject lines include:
•**[Colleague]** said we should connect
•Appropriate person
•quick question
•Question – **[Named Initiative]**
•**[Prospect]**, got time?
•**[Competitor]** just did…

PPOV Email: Body & Presumptive Close

Using *J.Barrow's* Why You, Why You Now (WYWN) strategy in the body of the email aligns with the mantra of relevance and personalization. SDRs should be using the research they do in every PPOV email they write.

WYWN can leverage the personal, company or industry level research. The point is that the email will apply to this specific prospect for a reason.

As previously discussed, you can vary the number of Value Points within an email to tailor to the cadence strategy. Generally, utilizing customer snippets, 2 sentence case studies, builds credibility and brings to life your product in action.

It brings credibility by showing specific ROI and similar customers that your company works with. Beyond the metrics, a great PPOV includes the impact on the business as a whole and how it made it more successful for the company and your product's champion.

One of the key deliverables for a great Marketing team will be to produce a customer snippet library as the go-to resource. For each profile in your company's ITP, there should be a relevant customer snippet for your SDRs to reference.

Lastly, a presumptive and specific close reduces the mental workload for a prospect to engage. Make it as easy as possible to say yes to a meeting. When prospects understand that all they have to do is reply with an affirmative and not have to get into a tet-e-tet to find a suitable time, they're much more likely to take action. Proposing multiple times is useful for this reason and email efficiency tools allow you to do this easily.

Email Type: The Follow-up Email
To ensure the value of a PPOV email is fully used, SDRs should send quick follow-up emails.

Often, prospects are simply busy or forget to respond to an email. The assumption should be that a PPOV provides value and deserves a response -- the SDR did in fact do a lot of research to ensure that the PPOV email was valuable after all!

A quick email with a few words can be an effective method to remind an executive or prospect that a response is expected. A simple "following-up" or "Wanted to make sure you got this." gets the message across and also lets the prospect know that the person on the other side of the email is actually a living, breathing human.

Again, changing the subject line to these emails to include or be replaced by "re:" can increase open rates without being disingenuous. I do not advocate this practice with initial PPOV emails, as this "tricks" prospects into opening emails and begins the customer journey on tenuous footing.

PPOV emails should provide enough value in the subject line and body to earn an open, and follow-up emails should simply be a reminder.

Email Type: The Break-up Email
Towards the end of a cadence, a break-up email can be a humorous way to re-engage a prospect.

This is a great opportunity for SDRs to incorporate their own personality into the sales process. The goal of a break-up email is to reassert previous PPOVs and to build a sense of urgency for the prospect to respond.

Here's an example break-up email for a competitor cadence:

Subject: did I do something wrong?

First Name,

Competitor isn't going away, but unfortunately I do have to get going soon! Let's make this easy; just respond back with a number:

1 - If you'd like a calendar invite to discuss how Competitor and us work together.

2 - If you're not interested right now.

Thanks!

--

Other break-up emails have included pictures of hippos, sports teams, bookshelves, quicksand, Jason Bourne and the "help, I've fallen but I can't get up!" lady.

Creativity and personality -- the world is your oyster on break-up templates.

Emails: Performance and Team Messaging

Effective ABSD email templates coupled with good prospecting can be expected to yield 40%+ open rates and 10%+ reply rates. That's 2x the effectiveness of the typical email marketing campaign. The best targeted cadences and templates can have 50%+ open rates. Tailored messaging matters.

Template metrics can be useful when comparing performance against a baseline, but should not be the end-all.

By understanding and enforcing the **principles** of effective emails, SDRs can be taught to be self-sufficient without having to rely on the templates that others develop which may or may not be relevant to their territory. Teach a man to fish instead of giving him one.

In the near future, more data on the effectiveness of whole cadences will allow SDRs to test not only content, but also strategy and intensity.

Although email template and cadence design should be centralized for core Industry, Use-Case and Catch-All cadences where performance is tried and true, SDRs should be empowered to build and deliver their own as well. Not only does this allow for more testing of better cadences when metrics do become available, but it is central to the challenge (and allure) of the enterprise SDR role.

For example, you or your Marketing team may not have the cycles (or knowledge) to develop a Financial Services cadence, but your SDR that covers New York might have the time to do so with the help of his AEs and a little elbow grease.

Additionally, with the ability to share cadences instantaneously, winning messaging can be quickly distributed to the entire team to execute the instant it is identified.

Once the Financial Services cadence is built and tested by your New York SDR, your London SDR would benefit from using the same messaging and strategy since his territory has many Financial Services firms. No need to reinvent the wheel.

Regular review and testing on template and cadence performance, along with distribution of best practices allows the **entire team** to continuously innovate. Since messaging needs to be tailored, it now needs to be done from both centralized and decentralized positions. Centrally built cadences ensure there's a core to scale, while decentralized cadences tailor into the details.

Prospecting is no longer for the wolves; it is now a team effort.

Part 5: Warm Calling

Nothing gets me more riled up than the idea that SDRs should be following a call script. What are they, robots?! What's the use in recruiting real, live humans when you could just hit record and play?

The SDR role is much more than simply "smiling and dialing".

SDRs take a proactive consultative approach in adding value. They use their research and knowledge of a contact, account and industry to provide value to prospects. SDRs should want to win a small 'trusted advisor' role within the account they are speaking to. This means understanding a prospect's goals and listening to their challenges and then mapping the company's solution to their needs.

Although "Cold Calling is Dead" has been a provocative theory for the past several years, it has too often been translated to "Calling is Dead." This is not true at all. Calling is still very much alive and well, however the purpose of calling someone has fundamentally changed.

Calling differentiates SDRs from the typical marketing email campaign - it informs the prospect that she is indeed being targeted by an actual human with value to provide. Leaving a voicemail does the same thing.

Calls also imply that an SDR highly values their prospect, and would take the time out of the day to reach out to them personally.

Calls positively impact the conversion of a cadence, and are a healthy part of cadence design, as long as they provide value by pursuing a PPOV.

Warm Calling: Response Times and Best Hours to Call
According to the often-cited Harvard Business Review study by Insidesales.com, the odds of contacting a lead if called in 5 minutes versus 30 minutes drop 100x. It is worth picking up the phone as soon as a lead comes in.
Additionally, the best times for calling are 8-9 in the morning and 4-6 in the afternoon local time.

Lastly, Wednesdays and Thursdays are the best days to call, while Mondays are often overloaded with meetings, making it hard to connect with people.

Warm Calling: Strategy

When first starting out, SDRs should intentionally set a goal for each of their calls. Not every call has to have the same goal, although the purpose of a prospecting *cadence* should always be to set a qualified meeting for the AE.

Example call goals:

- Scheduling a meeting
- Reminding someone to read your email
- Informing them you are a real person
- Implying that they are important to you
- Finding out who is in charge of XYZ

Straight cold calling surely is dead. SDRs should have a PPOV ready from their research on the contact, account or industry. To help them deliver these at scale, avoid context switching as much as possible. SDRs should schedule their call times to roll through a single PPOV during a set of calls in the same cadence - that way they don't have to mentally reset on a new PPOV with each new call.

For cold prospects, warm calling, which is following the delivery of a PPOV via email or LinkedIn is usually much more effective since the prospect has time to understand the context of the call. Once on the phone, they're more ready to discuss the topic and they have materials available to them to get up to speed.

Warm prospects should be followed up on immediately before they switch contexts and move on to their next task.

In general, people are busy and qualified warm prospects should get at least 6 calls. For qualified contacts, persistence not only pays off, but is often valuable to the prospect in order to remind them of their priorities.

The amount of effort should be directly related to how closely the account fits within the ideal target profile and the contact fits the definition of a mobilizer, which will be explored in detail later in this section.

Warm Calling: Call Criteria
Calls should be graded in the same manner as the role plays used to evaluate candidates earlier. Here's a quick reminder of the grading criteria:

- **Strength of Introduction**: SDRs should ask for time and demonstrate value early on.
- **Use of Customer Voice**: Use of case studies and success stories.
- **Qualification of Need / Open Questioning**: Obtained or tried to obtain enough information to gain a good understanding of prospect's need by using open questions.
- **Objection Handling**: Ability to handle obstacles like questions on pricing or competitors in a thoughtful and skillful manner. Should be able to direct the conversation back to their own agenda.
- **Presumptive Close**: Presumptive and effective close that clearly outlines the next appropriate action.
- **Active Listening**: Listen using affirmative verbal cues and rephrasing what is said in a thoughtful manner.
- **Tenacity**: Deal well with adversity and continue to pursue their goals on the call no matter what.
- **Originality**: Agility to creatively navigate the conversation in an articulate, positive and value-added manner.

Let's take a quick example of an SDR, Ailbhe, making a good phone call.

Ailbhe (Call Opening): Hi _____, Ailbhe Rees from COMPANY, did I catch you at a bad time?

Prospect: Always a bad time, but go ahead.

Ailbhe (Establish Rapport): I know! We're underwater here after Sales Kick-Off. I imagine y'all are going through the same thing?

Prospect: Sure are! SKO was intense. How can I help you?

Ailbhe (Upfront Contract + PPOV): Your LinkedIn profile showed that you are interested in providing data-driven insights through analytics. Here at COMPANY we're also passionate about that as the future of business, especially to optimize the supply-chain, which looks to be an area you specialize in. How are you currently using analytics to get insights about your supply chain?

Ailbhe (Retreat and Refer): (If not interested) Sounds like I'm a little lost. What do you focus on? Who would be the correct person to speak with about business intelligence or analytics?

Ailbhe (Qualify): (If interested) Great! (Asks more open-ended qualification questions) What are you trying to accomplish this year?

(Once qualification is vetted)

Ailbhe (Active Listening): Prospect, let me repeat back to you what I heard so we're sure I understand correctly. (Provide summary of notes).

Ailbhe (Customer Snippet): We have similar customers like XYZ who use us in that exact use-case. They've seen an increase in revenue by X%.

Ailbhe (Presumptive Close): Sounds like getting us running in your environment ASAP would be valuable to you. Let's schedule time for my product expert to go into more detail. He's worked with companies like A, B, C in your industry and can go into exactly how we deploy. He's available at these times next week X, Y, Z – when are you?

SDRs should then close with an attention to detail, re-confirming contact information and trying to expand the meeting to involve other stakeholders who would be involved in a potential evaluation.

Warm Calling: Voicemails

Voicemails can be used to indicate that the SDR is indeed a real person and can reference a PPOV as well. Although this is true, beware of leaving generic voicemails.

Anything that sounds "like a sales call" is really a prospect's manner of saying it sounds like "it's not well-researched and provides very little value."

So, just like building PPOV emails, make sure SDRs are ready to provide a verbal PPOV if they are leaving voicemails.

Example of a weak voicemail:
"Hi Steve, this is Ailbhe calling from COMPANY, the company behind PRODUCT. I just wanted to call you because I saw that you downloaded a white paper and I wanted to learn more about your project to see if I can offer you some helpful resources. Please give me a call back when you have time on XXX-XXX-XXXX. Thanks.

Example of a strong voicemail:
"Your CIO John Doe recently said that providing business insights via data-driven analysis was important and given your interaction with our website, I figured this was a good time to call. My name is Ailbhe from COMPANY. Give me a call back at XXX-XXX-XXXX. I'll shoot you an email a little later today, too."

Part 6: Bi-Modal Qualification

For years, sales development has been struggling to define a qualification scheme to match the rise of the informed buyer. We've started with BANT and moved to any number of other acronyms in search of the perfect set of qualification criteria. BANTE, BMANTR, ANUM...we've been trying desperately but are running out of letters.

What needs to be acknowledged, however, is that sales development is doing two very separate things: fulfilling demand and creating demand.

Each of these activities necessitates its *own* set of qualification criteria.

SDRs have to do both of these activities in order to create enough pipeline for our companies - leads in our ideal target profile won't double every year forever.

Fulfilling demand is reactive. Creating demand is proactive and deterministic. SDRs need to be able to identify both types of demand and qualify them, in essence Bi-Modal Qualification.

Bi-Modal Qualification: Fulfilling Demand
In standard fashion, fulfilling demand has not changed much. BANT still works -- much to the glee of old-fashioned salesmen everywhere. However, there is two problems with only pursuing demand that has already been created by the market.

The first problem is that you are much more likely to lose.

Remember, when a prospect has a project and has already scoped out their requirements, 70% of their journey is already done!

Most likely, another vendor has already manipulated the process in their favor. They've been in there for months -- crafting a vision, gaining stakeholders, helping their champion and driving the requirements. Your company faces an uphill battle to earn business as you answer the cattle call along with another 5-10 vendors.

Not only is winning their business difficult, but winning the amount of business you'd want (if you aim to become an enterprise platform) is shot because you are pigeon-holed into someone else's vision of what your product can or should do.

The second problem with only BANT qualifying and fulfilling demand is that there's only so much of it.

There are only so many projects in qualified accounts. If you wait around for prospects to educate themselves and get the guts to start a project, you'll be waiting forever. Most importantly, you forsake the ability to proactively craft the outcome in your territory.

Creating demand means propelling a compelling vision, developing personalized PPOVs, educating, enabling and arming mobilizers to make an impact within their organizations.

BANT qualified opportunities is a little like playing t-ball. It is basic. It doesn't move very much and you know how to deal with it. The problem is, you're probably not going to be hitting a home run with a t-ball anytime soon.

There's always a place for BANT, and as SDRs meet prospects with a project they should continue to qualify with it. But they have to be able to create demand as well.

Bi-Modal Qualification: Creating Demand

Taking a nod from *The Challenger Sale*, I've developed my own qualification criteria that run **in parallel** with traditional BANT qualification. Regardless of the criteria you develop for your group, the important part is to differentiate the two types of demand being created.

The sales organization has to be able to effectively prosecute **both** types of demand. The new Challenger qualification criteria is TPMC:

- T-Target Profile
- P-Provocative Point of View
- M-Mobilizer

- ## C-Commitment to Next Step

Challenger Qualification	Question	Additional Definition	Example Approved Notes
T - Target Profile	Ideal Target Profile (ITP) Qualification?	What transformation is the company going through that we can help resolve?	This is a large enterprise finance company with 5k employees and 3 million customers. They face an industry that is: -failing to monetize -heavy pressure to keep costs low -need to find new revenue streams -being disrupted by new technology (Mint, Venmo, etc.)
	Reason to Engage?	What is the prospect's initial interest? How did we engage with the prospect?	Prospect responded to outbound email through financial vertical focused cadence. Other, less qualified leads have been coming in around the account as well, so there may be awareness from the ground up.
	Potential Business Value - PPOV?	What is our PPOV on how the prospect can gain their desired outcome using us?	Prospect responded to a PPOV about finding new revenue streams and methods to monetize their customer data using sales analytics. Similar customer case studies: -GE -RBC
	Potential Business Impact - KPI/metric?	What specific outcome will this drive, as measured by quantifiable impact?	Increase customer conversion rate, customer lifetime value and $ generated.
P - Provocative Point of View	Current technology or data strategy?	What does the current strategy and environment look like? How does this need to shift to align with our vision?	This is a legacy shop with an eye towards moving to the cloud. Other key data systems include: -SFDC -Marketo -Hadoop
M - Mobilizer	Why are they a mobilizer?	Does the contact we are speaking to have the ability to create projects, have influence over decision makers or is a decision maker themselves?	This is the Chief Data Officer with responsibility for all of the company's data, along with a mandate to monetize it. According to his LinkedIn profile, he's "passionate about big data and data-driven decision making through analytics."
C - Commit	Committed Next Step?	Has the prospect committed to a next step that will further educate them on our vision?	Prospect agreed to and should see a demo of the product, along with meeting with RSD/SC team for technical evaluation of current data environment.

If BANT is playing t-ball, then with TPMC we're playing softball. The ball is moving a little faster, and it might be curving as it reaches home plate.

The SDR's job is to make the ball as big as possible by landing with the right people in the right accounts with the right PPOV.

Each AEs pipeline should have a healthy mix of both types of demand. Short-term transactional demand can pay the rent while AEs should be actively driving demand to go on safari and bring back an elephant or two. (Not OK with any actual elephant hunting.)

Part 7: Cross Functional Engagement

All because Sales Development is a discipline of its own doesn't mean that it can be successful without other parts of the organization.

Marketing, our key supplier of leads and target profile, must understand what is required of them be held accountable.

Sales, our key customer of opportunities and pipeline, must be aligned on strategy and qualification.

Beyond developing new business, SDRs can leverage the Customer Success team to further penetrate customer accounts in a Land and Expand strategy.

First, in order to build a scalable demand-generation machine, the relationship with Marketing is critical.

Marketing Operations & Demand-Gen

As discussed previously, execution of an automated lead architecture which gets leads to the right people in the least amount of time is critical to the success of Sales Development and a basic building block. This is the first and most important ask of Marketing.

For this reason, the relationship between Marketing Operations/Demand-Gen and Sales Development is the first key to cross-functional success. If the infrastructure is wrong, if the leads are poor, then Sales Development will be ineffective and starve.

A marketing operations team with the skill to execute and the vision to architect enables Sales Development success.

Product Marketing

Secondarily, Marketing needs to provide the Ideal Target Profile (ITP) for accounts and the Buyer Profiles for contacts. This accurately targets SDRs to understand what companies and who within those companies they should be prospecting into.

For instance, if your product solves complex enterprise-level challenges in sophisticated IT environments, the ideal target profile would be CIO's and IT organizations in Fortune 2000 accounts.

Understanding this, compensation and strategy can be appropriately set to weight prospecting in that direction. Although basic, a consistent and thorough ITP goes a long way. Further segmentation into verticals, technology or use cases help with targeting as well.

However, do not boil the ocean. SDRs can only retain a few ITPs and Buyer Profiles at a time -- staying within an ITP for a period of time will help SDRs to become more credible as they learn industry lingo and use cases.

The next thing that Marketing should be held accountable to providing is a list of short customer case studies, or snippets. These are two to three sentence description of how a customer uses your product and the value they derived from it.

Long-form whitepapers on a customer case study are generally useless to SDRs -- that's never going to fit into a readable email or within the context of a conversation with a time-sensitive mobilizer. It may be helpful later in the sales cycle, but brevity and clarity are the hallmarks of a great SDR.

Custom snippets should provide useful ammo in an SDR's back pocket, something they should memorize and be able to tell stories around. Linking a prospect's need to a successful customer in real-time is an easy and effective method of providing value above expectations.

A good customer snippet library should cover all of the ITP industry/use cases that have been identified. SDRs should then be asked to memorize the snippets which pertain to the ITPs which they have identified in their go to market strategy.

Campaigns & Field MRKT
Lastly, regular updates from Marketing on messaging, inbound leads and upcoming events keeps everyone on the same page. Having a

single Marketing liaison is extremely valuable, and they should meet regularly with SDR leadership.

Field MRKT engagement is also critical to mutual success, as great territory strategies use field events as a compelling event to drive prospect engagement.

MRKT In the Long Run

As the Marketing engine scales, there will be diminishing marginal returns on leads. You can't expect the number of quality leads to double every year along with your growth targets -- the world is only so big and traditional marketing can only reach so much of it.

That means that AE's must be able to translate executive engagement into real projects and that pricing must increase to reflect the additional value provided to prospects by doing so. Once conversion of MQLs reaches 7%+ and SALs up to 15%, there's not much more room to fiddle with the core demand-gen engine and focus must turn to creating growth through account penetration.

Marketing can help with account penetration as well, as product marketing and other thought-leaders can help to develop PPOVs for specific accounts that may be more insightful than a PPOV built by an SDR. Having additional resources researching accounts and building PPOVs will further leverage an SDR's effectiveness in delivering those messages to the right people at scale.

Field Sales

The field sales team is the customer for sales development, and should be treated as such.

That means providing a POV on how to approach each opportunity and listening to their feedback in order to improve.

The give-get relationship also means that SDRs should hold the field accountable to quickly following up with opportunities and prosecuting demand consistent with the sales methodology.

Setting an upfront contract with sales sets everyone up for success. The first step would be to identify the ITP and Buyer Profile, effectively targeting accounts and mobilizers together.

Also, agree with sales that if they are to pull additional resources from the company to work an opportunity, then it should be accepted as one. This ensures that resources are properly allocated and opportunities have the appropriate level of scrutiny from management. Every company has scarce resources to help close deals, only qualified opportunities should be supported with them.

I've had many conversations where sales wants a bucket in which they can throw "accepted" leads into, but have them unmanaged. This will make it easier to hit SAL numbers, but decreases sales accountability. Not a good tradeoff!

For instance, we once started our stages at "Stage 1 - 10%" but sales wanted to create "Stage 0 - 5%" as accepted in order to avoid accountability on accepted opps. Do not let this, or anything similar to this happen. Every step of the funnel must have accountability, ownership and visibility. Just one hole, like this "Stage 0 - 5%" can result in a drastic reduction in conversion rate as opportunities pile up there with no oversight.

To avoid this, tie qualification criteria to the sales methodology adopted by your organization. Set the upfront contract on what an opportunity looks like and deliver ruthlessly to meet that criteria. This holds both the SDRs and AEs to carrying out the company's sales methodology with consistent excellence.

The Account Penetration Team

SDRs are a part of a territory's account team and should be treated as such. They should be accountable to providing a quarterly business plan, and reporting their results on a weekly basis to their SDR manager, AEs and the RVP of their region. In return, the AEs and RVPs should bring them into the team's fold, provide strategic direction and mentor the SDR. The best RVPs manage their SDRs in a hands-on fashion, making them valuable resources to leverage within their team.

The relationship with their AEs is the most important relationship a SDR will have. They are a partner, customer, mentor and comrade in arms. Maintaining a feedback loop, mutual accountability and healthy, consistent relationship between the two sides is critical for their success.

As mentioned previously, pairing an SDR with 3 AEs within an RVP's territory will align the teams and create a stable recipe to crush quota. There is value to stability, once an SDR and AE pair prove successful, try not to tinker.

The early success of AEs can be directly tied to the pipeline they are able to generate. Having a pre-ramped SDR partner for new AEs to engage with can make them effective much more quickly. Experienced SDRs can help on-board new AEs.

Sales and SDR MGMT
In high-growth situations, communication between sales management and SDR management becomes critical. As Sales hires AEs, SDR management must be one-step ahead by hiring the required SDRs months before new AEs start.

Territory changes, qualification criteria, strategy tweaks and account ownership can be fluid and confusing without regular communication between Sales and SDR management.

Customer Success and Customer Development
Almost every SaaS company has a land and expand strategy.

Unfortunately, the expand portion of the strategy can often be overlooked as all the marketing, SDR and sales resources focus on landing new logos.

Customer Success is often tasked with up selling or cross-selling, but they generally are not incentivized to do so. Aggressively hunting for more sales within their accounts could also jeopardize their renewals. Customer Success Managers are also not usually natural sales hunters, they are more likely farmers.

However, customer accounts should be the lowest hanging fruit out there! What did we land for, if not to expand? Customers have already signed paper and probably have a very successful deployment. Why are we not leveraging this to drive a broader engagement and, possibly, a shorter sales cycle without the involvement of all the lawyers?

SDRs can work with CSMs anytime they decide to pursue a customer account. Customer Success can often be risk-averse in introducing SDRs to their accounts for fear of risking the renewal, their main KPI. To avoid this, SDRs should take note and avoid of any sensitive contacts/business units. They should also test and validate their PPOV with the CSM working the account.

Side Note: Customer Development Representatives

An alternative SDR role, the Customer Development Representative (CDR) can help fill this gap. CDRs, in essence, work just like SDRs except exclusively with customer accounts. CDRs fix the problem that AEs and CSMs don't prospect into customer accounts.

CDRs force the issue, creating opportunities and engagement within customer accounts that otherwise would be left dormant.

CDRs work more strategically across the CSM and AE organizations in order to better understand specific customer use cases, gain introductions and avoid at-risk accounts. However, they can be managed and compensated just like SDRs and should be a natural extension of the Sales Development team.

CHAPTER 10
THE FUTURE OF SALES DEVELOPMENT

Before this book ends, let's take a moment to stare into the future of the profession. I make 7 predictions in 2016 for Sales Development in 2026 and leave you with a challenge.

Part 1: The Future of Sales Development
Part 2: My Hope for You

Part 1: The Future of Sales Development

Prediction #1: Account-Based Sales Development will eat into Account-Based Marketing.

As ABSD and ABM mature, they will grow closer to each other. Content producers and sales development representatives are already working hand in hand to mold messaging for specific accounts.

It is not implausible that in the near future SDRs will produce content (blog posts, landing pages, social media), assets (info graphics, whitepapers, direct mailers) and events (guerilla marketing, field events, roadshows) for specific accounts on their own.

Enabled by rigorous training, a depth of knowledge and next-generation tools, SDRs will become a channel for valuable content all their own.

The further this goes, the closer SDRs will get to becoming Account-Based Marketers.

Prediction #2: Sales Development work will move off of Salesforce to another platform entirely. Salesforce will stay the system of record.

Like your great uncle, it's old, and hairy, and isn't going to change anytime soon. It's Salesforce.

The ability to effectively prospect and deliver cadences cannot be from within Salesforce. Plenty of smart people have tried, the architecture just doesn't support the functionality needed.

A prospecting and outreach platform that integrates with Salesforce will set the standard on Sales Development workflow. The ability to tailor at scale will necessitate an entirely different, next-generation platform.

Salesforce will not be replaced as the system of record and CRM (it's in too deep to perform open-heart surgery), but a new sales platform will emerge that actually helps salespeople sell. It will be our ally, helping to build, organize and deliver cadences.

It will do deep research into the web to bring in relevant account and contact specific information so SDR's can write emails and make effective phone calls more quickly. It will suggest content and messaging based on the profile of the accounts or contacts selected. By combining web crawling with internal content, the platform will offer *predictive messaging*. It will help SDRs by suggesting PPOVs and build entire cadences based on the group's real performance analytics.

There will be a portal for collaboration with internal SMEs on messaging, content and assets. Robust analytics and rigorous testing methods will ensure that not only will email templates be measured, but entire cadences, phone calls, voicemails and keywords.

This platform will stand alone from Salesforce (or any CRM), but will integrate with CRMs via an API.

This will effectively separate the housing of sales data with the workflow that produces it.

Prediction #3: SDR leaders will use automated data analysis to coach and forecast in real-time.

An integrated gamification, performance management, sales analytics and 1:1 platform will change the way leaders coach and manage their teams.

With the drastic increase in sales data collected, leaders will need help with the ability to interpret all of the data and turn those insights into actionable steps. In the future, a software platform will be able to automatically detect what an SDR is doing well (or not so well) by comparing performance against industry and team baselines.

If an SDR is not being effective - with low conversion rates on his cadences, the platform will be able to identify why by comparing the email templates he uses against those of his peers and the content or duration of his calls. It will be able to point out to his coach that his subject lines are too long or that his calls are too short. It will then shoot over a recording of sample calls for coach analysis.

This platform will also be able to see if an SDR's effort is keeping up with the team's commitment or baseline. It will notify players and coaches if the volume of activity is abnormally high or low. It will also calculate the effective conversion rate needed for that lower level of activity to result in quota attainment or anticipate performance over quota if a high-level of activity is sustained.

All of this analysis will be pushed to both the player and coach via email, web application and mobile notification in a daily Automated Analytics Report (AAR). AARs will form the foundation of 1:1s. Coaches will continue to provide human interpretation, while assigning and tracking actions that will most efficiently lead to blowing out quota.

Forecasting will be more precise than ever before. It will be done via several models, one of which will be updated in real-time based on the *anticipated* activities and conversion rates based on historical data.

Prediction #4: Advanced sales analytics will begin measuring SDR Efficiency Rating (SER) and an SDR shot chart.

This same advanced analytics work will be pushed out the entire team to track not only volume, but effectiveness. It will no longer be enough to produce a high volume of activity, but to produce a high-volume of **effective** activity that converts into positive results. Leaderboards will go from strict volume, to include efficiency.

The movement to measure basketball players purely by Points-Per-Game (PPG) changed the day Player Efficiency Rating (PER) came into being. It's a lot less impressive that it takes Kobe Bryant 20 shots to score 10 points at the end of his career in 2016, when it only took him 10 shots to do the same thing during his prime in 2006. He's much less efficient as he grows older and when he has a higher usage rate (running more plays).

Here are the top 10 players in PPG so far this season (2016) according to ESPN.

PLAYER	TEAM	PTS[4]	PER[5]	PTS RK	PER RK	PTS v PER
Stephen Curry, PG	GS	29.7	32	1	1	0
James Harden, SG	HOU	28	25.33	2	7	-5
Kevin Durant, SF	OKC	27.7	28.09	3	3	0
DeMarcus Cousins, C	SAC	27	23.53	4	10	-6
LeBron James, SF	CLE	25	26.99	5	4	+1
Damian Lillard, PG	POR	25	22.88	5	14	-9
Anthony Davis, PF	NO	24.3	25.98	7	5	+2
Russell Westbrook, PG	OKC	24	28.95	8	2	+6
DeMar DeRozan, SG	TOR	23.4	21.22	9	26	-17
Paul George, SF	IND	23.2	20.25	10	40	-30

On first glance, you would assume each of these players is elite. You can see PER tells a slightly different story for players like Paul George, who should probably be taking less shots.

In sales development, activity volume (usage rate) and effectiveness (efficiency) will be needed to measure a more holistic view of performance. The ability to measure the effectiveness of each SDR (down to his emails, cadences, assets used and calls) will shed light on the effective conversion rate for each of his activities, just like a shot chart.

---

[4]http://espn.go.com/nba/statistics/player/_/stat/scoring-per-game/sort/avgPoints/year/2016/seasontype/2

[5] http://insider.espn.go.com/nba/hollinger/statistics

Sticking with basketball, this is Stephen Curry's 2013 shot chart:

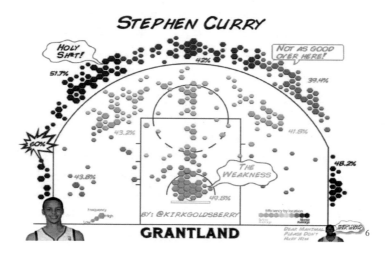

Steph saw that he was particularly weak near the bucket, a below average player at finishing near the rim. Using this data, Steph worked on his game and this is Stephen Curry's MVP-winning 2015-2016 shot chart:

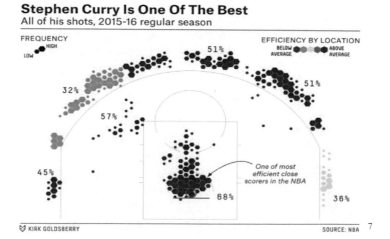

---

[6] http://grantland.com/the-triangle/courtvision-just-how-good-are-stephen-curry-and-klay-thompson/

[7] http://fivethirtyeight.com/features/stephen-curry-is-the-revolution/

Using data to identify his biggest weakness turn it into his biggest strength, Steph transformed his game to reach the next level. He led his team to the 2015 NBA Championship and began a basketball revolution.

Collecting similar data in a sales shot chart will create real-time actionable insights for sales people and their coaches. It will also create a baseline to measure SDR performance company-wide and down to a granular level. Coaches will be able to better compare SDR performance on specific skills and activities, across groups.

Driven by data-driven coaching, more SDRs will blow out quota more quickly than ever before. Quotas and productivity will rise by at least 30%. A 13x SDR Multiple will be the new standard.

Prediction #5: Account-Based Sales Development will be table stakes, and Contact-Based Sales Development will begin.

As ABSD becomes widely adopted, the ability to differentiate messaging will once again move to a more granular level. The arms race to provide more value than the next vendor will not end at the account level.

Real personalization will occur; entire cadences and marketing campaigns will target one specific contact at a time.

Prospects will receive more value from their vendors than ever before. Individualized content, agendas, landing pages and assets will be mass produced and delivered at exactly the right moment.

SDRs will be the ones crafting, tailoring and delivering these campaigns.

Prediction #6: Sales Development leaders will earn their place at the executive level.

It will be the norm for a Sales Development leader to be a part of the executive team. The function will mature and become professionalized.

Investors, CEOs and Boards will realize the importance of an independent and successful Sales Development organization. They will scour the market for talented Sales Development leaders in the same way they search for a great CMO, CFO or Head of Sales.

A few Chief Sales Development Officers (CSDOs) will exist in forward-looking companies.

Prediction #7: More executives will have a background in Sales Development.

The wave of talent trained in today's SDR nurseries will go on to be the next wave of tech talent.

Those young professionals have now turned into an army of well-trained high-achievers across the technology landscape that will support the SDR cause because that is where they got their start, it is where they built their foundation.

Eventually, these same talented individuals will be the future CEOs, CMOs, SVPs and founders. They will find their success using the core skills and philosophy they developed as enterprise SDRs.

Part 2: My Hope for You

The Sales Development business model can bring massive, predictable scale to any software company. It also has the opportunity harness the raw talent of a new generation to make unicorn companies much more common.

Building MuleSoft's Sales Development organization may have been difficult, but that doesn't mean it can't be done again. It is repeatable. I am sure that others can duplicate and improve upon our success - and are doing so already.

My hope is that after reading this book, you are one step closer to investing in your own Sales Development unicorn, one that leaves everyone else in the dust and expands the universe of Sales Development success stories.

My hope is that you can positively impact the lives of hundreds of young professionals.

My hope is that you bring leadership to the fledgling and nascent industry we call Sales Development

And when you do, my hope is that you give back to our budding profession...our young community.

I can't wait to hear what you come up with.

My hope **is** you.

TLDR?

- **Sales Development has become a discipline**. Sales Development's core competency is finding, creating, and qualifying demand. This has become a highly specialized skill which requires its own professional management.
- **An ounce of Sales Development covers a multitude of sins**. Sales Development creates money for the business consistently and at scale. For every $1 invested, Sales Development can return 10x.
- **Like College Football coaches, Sales Development matures raw talent into professionals.** Sales Development coaches a new generation into Technology and bridges the gap from the academic world to the professional.
- **Sales Development is the engine to creating linear, predictable demand at Unicorn Scale.** While other revenue streams may experience diminishing marginal returns, SDRs can scale pipeline linearly.

ABOUT THE AUTHOR

Chris Pham is the Sr. Director of Global Sales Development at Birst. Before joining Birst, he founded the Sales Development team at MuleSoft, a privately held +$1.5B company on Forbes' List of Unicorns.

From Tempe, Arizona - Chris graduated from The Wharton School of Business at the University of Pennsylvania with a concentration in Management.

He's an avid fan of Anthony Bourdain, (allegedly) cheating at Settlers of Catan, good music and Soul-cycling.

Chris is most passionate about developing the people and community around him. He hopes to see the people he has impacted go on to live fulfilling lives as leaders of positive change and giving.

30832317R00095

Made in the USA
Middletown, DE
08 April 2016